The House of Atreus

MINNESOTA DRAMA EDITIONS NO. 2 · EDITED BY TYRONE GUTHRIE

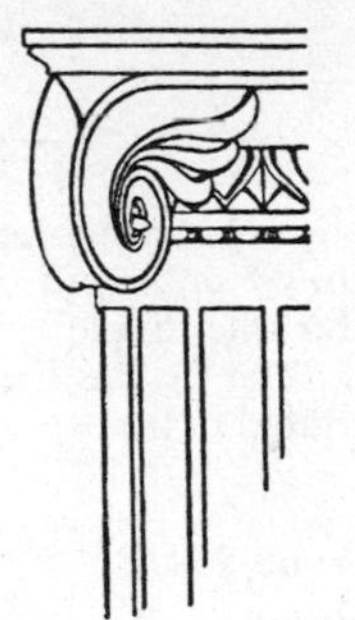

AESCHYLUS

THE HOUSE OF ATREUS

ADAPTED FROM THE

Oresteia

BY JOHN LEWIN

MINNEAPOLIS · THE UNIVERSITY OF MINNESOTA PRESS IN
ASSOCIATION WITH THE MINNESOTA THEATRE COMPANY

Library of Congress Catalog Card Number: 66-27418

PUBLISHED IN GREAT BRITAIN, INDIA, AND PAKISTAN BY THE OXFORD UNIVERSITY PRESS, LONDON, BOMBAY, AND KARACHI, AND IN CANADA BY THE COPP CLARK PUBLISHING CO. LIMITED, TORONTO

The House of Atreus

The Adapter's View of The House of Atreus

by JOHN LEWIN

MY AIM in writing this English version of the *Oresteia** has been twofold: first, since the script is designed for contemporary stage presentation (as was the original), to make it as theatrically workable and dramatically effective as possible; second, since English needs no apologies, in comparison either with classical Greek or with any other language, to make the English as direct, poetically powerful, rich, and flexible as it was within my ability to do, lapsing neither into journalese flatness nor into self-conscious archaisms. (At times, however, even archaisms seem to me dramatically appropriate: the language of Clytemnestra's speeches to Agamemnon in which she attempts to persuade him to walk on the purple (page 31) may be treated as genuinely stately rather than as self-parodying, but at the cost of missing a terrible irony. She is not merely persuading him to the sin of hubris but, in human terms, consciously endeavoring to make the last memory of him which his soldiers and subjects will have that of a ridiculous ass, a gorgeously vulgar Asiatic tyrant, rather than that of a grizzled giant seamed by trouble and responsibility and simple as a sword blade.)

All very well. But the inescapable question will arise: is it Aeschylus? Admittedly, this version is not a faithful and reverent subordination of the adapter's imagination to the letter of the original.

* The name usually given to the trilogy. The title *The House of Atreus* was suggested by Sir Tyrone Guthrie, who commissioned the work for production by the Minnesota Theatre Company, as an indication of the nature of this version—a free adaptation rather than a literal translation.

The procedure of the actor, director, designer, composer, and all others concerned with converting a written text into a full-scale stage production involves more than a merely physical change; it is, strictly speaking, a chemical transmutation, and whether the result is gold or dross can be judged only by concrete results, not by theoretical principles or abstract values. This procedure, as well as I can describe it, consists of breaking down the words of the text into the immediate nonverbal situations for which they are a code or formula, distilling these through the imagination, and transforming them into the complex of visual and auditory patterns of which a production consists. It is readily apparent that the result will be quite different from that of reading the text in the privacy of one's study, and herein lies a certain risk: that, since the values of the theatre are not those of the study, shifts of emphasis and interpretation will occur which may be considered by some to be illuminations and by others gross distortions of the playwright's meaning.

Has a translator or adapter, insofar as he is a poet and/or a man of the theatre, license to take similar liberties—even to the extent of interpolations? I have, for example, introduced several lines not to be found in any Aeschylean text into Athena's explanation of the basis for her decision (page 104). I can only hope that this is not equatable with the insertion of a clock in the Venus de Milo's midsection; but the necessity in this case, and at other points where similar changes have been made, has seemed to me sufficiently clear. It must be apparent to anyone concerned with living art that certain images from the cultural tradition, the "great starry harvest of five thousand years," to paraphrase Blake's figure, have been enriched and certain ones diminished by the contingencies of time. To the "ideal" reader, or playgoer, as familiar with the intellectual, social, moral, and theological currents of Hellenic culture as with those of his own milieu, there will be no problem, and he doubtless will become impatient with those who suggest that there might *be* a problem. But the audience of Aeschylus' own time was not an intellectual elite, and it is neither reasonable nor realistic to expect that audiences of today will be.

The English-speaking world has seen few performances of the trilogy as a whole—a strange fate if the *Oresteia* is a compellingly exciting unit rather than a pair of embarrassingly dull and obscure afterpieces tacked on to the *Agamemnon.* Length may be one reason, but I suspect that another is a certain doubt about the relevance of the *Oresteia*'s cumulative "point." To make the *Agamemnon* anything but thrilling requires an unusual capacity for obtuseness, but by the time one has reached *The Furies* (*Eumenides*) one has passed from the guts to the mind, and if the point of this culminating play is made to seem trivial or truistic the translator or adapter has confessed his lack of faith in the genius of Aeschylus and raised the question of why he bothered to translate him at all.

It behooves the translator or adapter to be quite clear in his own mind what he believes this point to be, and, in the light of this, what elements should be emphasized. If only Aeschylus' recording of a historical *fait accompli,* the transition from justice by vendetta to justice by jury trial and the law of the *polis,* is important, then modern audiences, especially conditioned as they are to themes of the denial of the voices of the blood by the establishment of *too much* order, will become justifiably restless. Moreover, scholars have spoken rather wistfully of the fact that the law and justice established is only for the city of Athens and those city-states (such as Argos) with which Athens happened to be negotiating alliances at the time, and that present concerns with "one world or none" have rendered this concept sadly dated.

The timelessly relevant hook with which to catch the contemporary mind is, I think, double-pronged. There is, first, the position given by Athena (wisdom) to the forces of nature, instinct and the unconscious (represented by the Furies and opposed by Apollo, lord of light, order, and Old Testament rectitude), within the organism of human society: neither repressed nor chaotically undisciplined, but occupying as valid a place as the concepts of reason and justice. Second, the play allows us to see the expansion of this concept of justice, and of human responsibility generally, to include not only "Us" but "Them," not only those to whom our loyalties fall naturally, as by mutual interests, ties of blood, common citizenship, or similar comfortable bonds, but those with whom we feel nothing in common, or with whom we disagree, and whose right to exist we "naturally" and self-righteously deny.

The Flies, Jean-Paul Sartre's drama of existential anguish and the terrible freedom of choice, is based on the *Oresteia* of Aeschylus. In the older play, the ultimate responsibility is shifted on to Athena, and even she, in a sense, is able to refer it upward to Zeus. In Sartre's version, Orestes himself is left with the full burden, and the point is made that to attempt to relieve himself of its weight would be an act of bad faith, an abnegation of his humanity. We are no longer able, at least not with the certitude of former times, to maintain that only a god or goddess can interrupt that remorseless, self-centered game of perpetual retribution by which men destroy themselves and each other. But we still find the majority of mankind eager to disclaim responsibility for their actions, to plead the determinism of an inexorable process of cause and effect, the dictates of the id and the superego. Sad to state, the suggestion that the process may be interrupted at all is still as revolutionary as it was in 458 B.C.

Aeschylus wrote the trilogy at a crucial point in the evolution of human thought, a time of transition, and for this reason alone we may find ourselves "resonating" with it more than with many another work written between his time and ours. An example of this is found in one of the central issues of the trilogy, the question of sanction of moral values, and hence, of courses of action based on those values. What is right action, and how is man to decide when the choice seems to be not between right and wrong, but between two rights? To detail the maddeningly intricate pattern of conflicts of right in the trilogy would occupy an entire thesis. Let us choose one example, that of Agamemnon's sacrifice of his daughter Iphigenia. To fulfill the vengeance of the gods on Troy, and to avoid the vengeance of the gods on his men, he must bring the vengeance of the gods (with Clytemnestra as the eventual instrument) upon himself. No doubt it is the Curse of Thyestes that has brought him to this plight, but the human situation which it represents has been experienced to some degree by all men. The Judeo-Christian answer is simple: because there is only one God, rather than a whole pantheon, there is only one truth, and only one valid sanction on human conduct, rather than the conflicting claims of many "rights." Theology today is grappling with the "death" of the Judeo-Christian God, or at least of those aspects of God that are patently the results of wish-fulfillment or rationalization. Sartrean existentialism concerns itself with the question of moral choice without "divine" moral guideposts, and the results, dramatically, are much the same as the conflicts in Aeschylus' trilogy. The evolutionary phases of human thought, from the dark forces of instinct, The Furies, to the arrogant light of consciousness exemplified by Apollo, and on through the true wisdom of synthesis and balance seen in Athena, are each sanctioned in their turn by the will of Zeus, and thus the development of man's concept of Deity is mirrored in dramatic images.

Our contemporary experience of the breaking up of values which we have consciously accepted for many centuries may foreshadow a renewal of the timeless "archetypal images" (as Jung calls them) by which the "world-soul" and the human psyche are brought into harmonious working. If Aeschylus' intuition of the operation of this awesome process in his time can be even partly realized for our own time, this adaptation will have served its purpose.

A Version for the Stage

by TYRONE GUTHRIE

I WRITE as one whose task will shortly be to stage the first production of this adaptation of the *Oresteia.* Let me say why we have preferred it to the many other versions which exist, some of them by scholars of the highest eminence. Many of these versions are more faithful both to the literal meaning of the original and to the distinctively Hellenic spirit. But it has seemed to us that such fidelity was not necessarily the supreme virtue for a stage version.

It is possible to conceive of a translation which would be utterly faithful; in which the literal meaning and the supraliteral "spirit" of every word, every phrase, would be conveyed into intelligible English. Such a version would not fail to be intensely interesting to a careful, patient, and well-prepared scholar; but it could rather easily fail to be musical. In performance, the music of verse is almost as important in conveying its meaning as is the syntax.

Verse translation which interestingly and faithfully conveys the meaning of an original poem is not always musical; if it is not, it is almost impossible to speak it intelligibly, let alone interestingly. Therefore we decided that a version which seemed to us highly musical should have preference over translations which, to a classical scholar, might seem more "faithful."

Inevitably in the course of two and a half thousand years many of the glories of a work of art must tarnish. To us, for instance, the stories are no longer as familiar as they were to the audiences who first saw these plays. We need to be reminded of the grisly facts of the Thyestean Feast; Agamemnon and Menelaus are not to us familiar symbols of dynasty; we even have to remind ourselves of the different theological significances of Zeus, Athena, Apollo, and Dionysus. Thus in grappling with the background we have to expend a certain amount of energy which can be ill spared from persons and events and ideas in the foreground.

Again, the various names of persons, and even of places, cannot have for us the same overtones which they must once have had. The great speech in which Clytemnestra describes the beacons flaming from mountaintop after mountaintop is still thrilling for us, because it is a thrilling idea. But how much more so when the mountains were familiar features of a beloved landscape, each name loaded with associations, memories, emotions!

To a limited number in a modern audience a few of the Greek place-names perhaps mean something: Hymettus, Kithairon, Marathon; just as to a few, a very few, Americans Flodden or Glencoe will evoke something of the associations which move the Scot. What, I wonder, will be the emotions evoked two thousand years from now, say in Tibet, by emotion-fraught American place-names like Gettysburg, Walden Pond, or Dallas?

Very little is known about how the original performances of Greek tragedy *sounded.* From the evidence of sculpture and architecture, we have some ideas of how they must have *looked.* Their music can only be imagined in the inadequate terms which study of a written text permits. The music of a modern performance must, therefore, largely be invented.

In the production of the *Oresteia* to be staged by the Minnesota Theatre Company we shall make some experiments with choral speech and try to bridge the gap between verse-speaking and singing. Speech, we hope, will merge imperceptibly into song.

Since choral speech, however carefully directed and laboriously rehearsed, is hard for an audience to follow, the choral lyrics must be cast in a form easily intelligible to a modern audience—familiar rhythms, short, clear sentences. Frequently this means changing the meter and simplifying the matter of the original. Occasionally it has been felt that, where the original supplied both narrative information and philosophic comment, often simultaneously, a simpler approach was necessary; the comment of the chorus has been made less philosophic and is, in general, a lyric interlude between the dramatic episodes.

In brief, our performance will make an endeavor to suggest the removed grandeur of the archetypal events and persons presented. In doing so, we shall make use of some of the devices which the Greek theatre is known to have used—not only choral speech but impersonal masks and so on. But we shall not use these devices in order to try to reconstruct the sort of impressions which an Athenian audience may have felt twenty-five hundred years ago.

The classical scholars in our audience will be asked to forget, if they can, their preconceptions. Let them look with twentieth-century eyes, listen with twentieth-century ears, and judge by what they see and hear, not by how closely it approaches, or how far it falls short of, their own learned, but primarily literary, notions about the *Oresteia*. Rather let them consider whether the archetypal situations have been re-created in a manner which makes an interesting and vivid theatrical event.

ACT I

Agamemnon

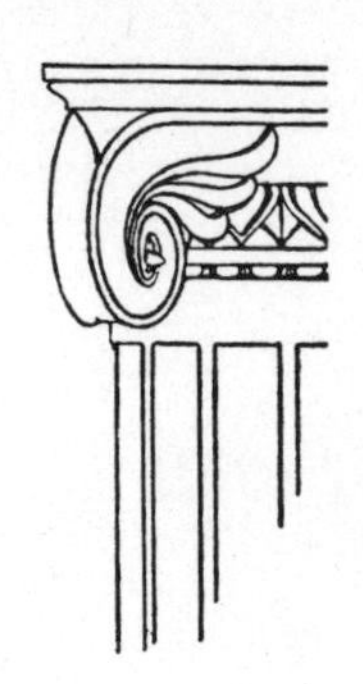

Characters

WATCHMAN
CLYTEMNESTRA
HERALD
AGAMEMNON
CASSANDRA
AEGISTHUS
CHORUS OF ARGIVE ELDERS
SOLDIERS, SERVANTS

Scene

Argos. The palace of Agamemnon. In the foreground, an altar.

(*It is just before dawn. There is a watchman on the roof.*)

WATCHMAN

O gods, give me an end to this chilly watch.
It drags on with the dying year while I
Crouch like a dog above the house of Atreus
Watching the marching armies of the stars,
The summer battalions and winter companies;
But of that other host, no news.
A flash of fire and I will know the job is done,
Troy town is taken, my king makes for home,
And I can come down from this hard and dew-wet bed,
Where that man-hearted woman who rules the palace
has placed me,
And sleep, perhaps, with sweet dreams.
But not now. No. Fear is up here with me
And no man sleeps that shares a bed with her.
I sing in the dark, but it sounds like weeping
When I think of this great house, what once it was
And how it is managed now.
(*singing*)
Bring good luck, immortal gods,
Throw the dice, but grant us odds—
(*He sees a light in the distance*)
They've lit thc beacon! It's done!
Queen! Town! Wake up!
Light the fires! Break out the wine! They're coming home!
Troy is down! Look! I'll start the dancing myself!
(*lights and movement in and beyond the palace*)
O gods, let it all turn out well.

Let me see my master again; put his hand back on
the reins.
The other things—let me not think of them.
I cannot speak; an ox stands huge on my tongue.
If the stones of that palace could talk, you would
hear a tale.
Until then—if you can, fill in my thoughts.
If not, forget even these few words I have said.
(*He exits. Enter the Chorus.*)

CHORUS

Ten years since Agamemnon and Menelaus,
The twin bronze fists of the house of Atreus,
Led forth a thousand ships to the doom of Troy.
The cry of war that rose from the throats of the Greeks
Was like the eagles' scream when their nest is found
Empty, their young taken away.
And as Apollo, Pan, or Zeus,
Hearing that song of blood high in the air,
Rolls the rock of Justice down on the transgressor,
So the house of Atreus rolled on to crush the house
of Priam.
For one woman and her loose love
The long line of man's flesh stood among the
hacking swords,
Straining muscle to muscle and knowing rest
Only when eyes darkened and knees struck the dust.
Greek and Trojan are caught on the Great Wheel,
And it will not be stopped by flame of altar or
water of eyes
Until the anger of the high gods is satisfied.
Meanwhile we wait, the empty of honor, the stay-at-homes,
Half-existing, as a dream remembered by day;
Babies that crawl on four feet, we that totter on three,
(*Clytemnestra enters*)
While the men that stand on two are gone
To kill and die in the fields at high-walled Troy.

But you, Clytemnestra,
Lady of Argos, wife of Agamemnon our lord,
Surely you have news. Has a change come?
You have commanded the altars to burn with constant
fire
All over our city, consuming holy oil
From the deep vaults of the royal treasury.
The high gods snuff up the pleasant smoke.
Surely this augurs well. If you have something to
tell us, speak.
(*Without answering, she re-enters the palace*)
I sing that day of gold and thunder when the
youth of the world
Shook the mane of his bronze helmet into the sun
And laughed like a horse at the patient and
narrow grave;
When the roadstead blackened with lean and shark-
nosed ships
Scenting the distant blood of Troy.
Then to the captains and kings an omen appeared:
On the right hand, the hard hand that holds the
scepter and spear,
Two eagles fell from the sky, one black as iron,
one blazed with silver,
And struck at a running hare. In a spray of blood
They tore the wet blind young from her swollen belly.
Sorrow is great: may good come out of it all.

Calchas the prophet-priest knew the eagles to be
Agamemnon and Menelaus, sharers of one fierce heart,
And thus he made clear the sign: From coping-stone
to corner-stone the belly of Troy
Will be ripped by the savage ram, and the Argive host
Will feed upon blood and gold, on flesh and wine.
But Artemis, the huntress of wild beasts,
Is their protector, and her holy heart

Shall swell with pity for the helpless prey,
And the winged hounds of her father, their pinions
sticky with blood,
Must fear her wrath and the high clear song of her bow.
Sorrow is great; may good come out of it all.

For she is tender and kind
To the young things of wood and meadow, the harmless hare
And the mighty lion;
But Artemis, protector of wild beasts,
Is their fierce huntress, and the omen must be fulfilled.
A young and helpless thing
Must fall to the iron talons, and the sweet earth
Must be watered with blood to cause fair winds to blow.
Thus the dark words of Calchas. Apollo our trust,
You see how men may be caught in a double snare,
Damned if we tug to the right, and damned if we pull
to the left,
Drowning in blood whichever way we turn.
Apollo, break the circle and show us a way:
Sorrow is great: may good come out of it all.

Almighty Zeus, whatever your secret name,
God omnipotent, do not turn away.
My own brain's light cannot pierce the darkness,
And I must turn to you if ever I am to know.
You have ordained that knowledge is bought with sorrow,
But ignorance of this hanging, voiceless threat
Is sorrow also.
O Zeus, if there is joy, then show her face to us;
If there is doom, do not let us meet him in the dark.

LEADER

On that day in Aulis
When no ship sailed
And the armed men sickened
In a foul wind,

The great seer Calchas
Spoke such words
That the tears of kings
Blew cold in the wind.

Then Agamemnon
Was torn in heart,
For the ships must rot
For want of a wind,

Or his daughter must die
On the altar-stone
To fill the sails
With a Troyward wind.

He chose his course:
They bared her throat
To the gleaming knife:
She cried in the wind

Her father's name:
They gagged her mouth:
No curse must fall
On man or wind;

The vision passes,
I see no more,
The voice of the god
Is lost in the wind.

(*Clytemnestra enters*)

CHORUS

Say no more; we shall see what is to come when it comes;
until then, let us not ask for misery.
Knowledge will come whether we want it or not;
Leave today to itself; tomorrow will make everything clear.
We must speak only of good, as she who protects our land
would desire,
Our lady here, Clytemnestra.

LEADER

Great Queen, I beg again, if you know that which we do not know, let us hear it.
We can only ask you humbly, and if you wish not to speak, so be it.

CLYTEMNESTRA

You shall have it all.
This was a night blessed above all other nights,
For on it Troy fell, and there is a great king who has seen his last dawn.

CHORUS

You said—can I believe—no!—Say that again!

CLYTEMNESTRA

Our armies hold Troy. Is that plain enough for you?

CHORUS

But—there have been so many rumors—what proof—

CLYTEMNESTRA

Do you accuse a god of lying?

CHORUS MEMBER

This is a dream. It can be no other.

CLYTEMNESTRA

You think of me, perhaps, as some greensick girl?

CHORUS

But what kind of messenger can come with so great speed?

CLYTEMNESTRA

A god I said, and a god it was.
The god of fire leaped the night-shrouded valleys
From peak to peak, and beacons cold these long years
Burned under the hands of joyful men
On Ida, Lemnos, Athos, and over the great sea;
And on Macistus, men whose eyes had strained long years
Until they saw false fires saw the true one
Leaping toward them, and lit their beacons in turn,

So that a current of flame streaked across the waters
    of Euripus
And the laughing watchmen on Messapius' hills
Heaped high the heather, and a crackle of orange fire
Made the god laugh too, in joyful strength
Increased, and he soared and swung like a scytheman
Across a frosty harvest of stars, and touched with light
The cold valleys of Asopus, and shone on Kithaeron
Like the autumn moon. The great marsh of Gorgopis felt
    his power
As the god raced on to Aegyplanctus' peak.
A hot spark struck amongst the high-stacked pine
And the god laughed again, and shook his beard of flame,
And leaped headlong across the Saronic Gulf,
Until last on Arachnus the great torch burst into bloom
And the flames fell on the house of Atreus, bringing
    news of joy.
There is my proof.
What have you to say now?

CHORUS

Nothing but thanks to the gods for this great day,
And wonder.
Feed my heart with more such news, if more you know.

CLYTEMNESTRA

I know only what must be, now:
The look of things in Troy.
Women lie crying on the hacked corpses
Of those that lay with them in love;
Children shake the stiff bodies
Of those that bore them, crying old sweet names
From throats that soon will be collared with the
    slave's iron.
But the Argives, drugged already with blood
And weary from the last great fight on the citadel wall,
Have ground out the spark of strength

On the bodies of once-proud women, and filled
their throats
With a wine of which no more will ever be drunk,
And now sleep like children
In soft beds without owners,
No more standing the nightly guard
Or lying open-mouthed to the icy stars.
But let them be satisfied.
The people and the city
Are crushed by the wheel. Let them go no further
And lay violent hands on the property of gods.
Leave the shrines standing, soldiers of Argos,
Or the gods may reach out as you go over the sea.
But yet there is blood in the earth that will cry
for blood;
There is wrong done with the knife, and though the
gods smile,
There are those of the dead who will not let old
wrongs sleep.
—You see me, elders of Argos, a timorous woman,
But one whose dearest wish is that right prevail.

LEADER

And no man could speak more wisely.
(*Clytemnestra exits*)
Now let us praise the gods for this,
For the joy was worth the pain.

CHORUS

O Father Zeus,
Your net of darkness
Is cast on Priam
And Priam's son:
A dreadful beauty
That gives me wonder:
You bow is bent
And justice done.

For those whose feet
Tread down the holy,
In no great house
Is any room
Whose doors ring not
To the knock of Justice,
No gold yet minted
To buy off doom.

That arrogant boy
The son of Priam
That spat on kindness
And shamed his host—
For him high Troy
Was damned with beauty
And Hellas armed
For a lovely ghost.

Tonight in Hellas
Will hear great weeping.
All over Troy
The corpse-fires burn:
Those who were tall
In youth and valor
Are homeward borne
In a little urn.

The people mutter
Against great leaders;
Blood will have blood;
The high may fall;
The ghosts of those
Who died for nothing
Will walk and wail
By a ruined wall.

CHORUS MEMBER

So, it seems, we cannot keep the shadows back.

LEADER

Only because we doubt the light.

CHORUS MEMBER

Why depend on false hopes?
If they are disappointed, it would not be the first time.

LEADER

We have the queen's word.

CHORUS MEMBER

Did she not say she is only a timorous woman?
Women believe what they want to believe, and are we such fools as to call hope and fear arbiters of truth?

ANOTHER CHORUS MEMBER

Look there! A herald coming from the shore!

LEADER

Now we shall know the reality for what it is,
And whether to laugh with joy or—

CHORUS

No! No!

LEADER

No, I would not have said it.
Things are too delicately balanced
To disturb them with evil words.

CHORUS

Oh, let all be well.

LEADER

Yes, let all be well.
He who would wish other for our city,
Give him what he richly deserves.
(*Enter the Herald*)

HERALD

O God, this good soil of Argos!
I thought this strange filth that covers me
Would cover my bones also.
Now I am home.

Even the sunlight is better here than in other lands.
A man can lose everything in ten years:
Health, friends, every illusion gone,
But kind are the gods who have given me my one wish:
To come home.
Apollo, I hope everything is all right between us.
By Scamander Water you were not good to us.
Our old quarrel is groundless now: there is no more Troy.
Great Agamemnon, who even now beaches on the shore,
His black ship whirled here by the storm-wind,
Has exacted full justice.
That golden city now looks
Like a dumping place for cinders and burnt bones.
The land is sterile, her seed dead,
The altars of her gods smashed to dust,
(*The Chorus reacts. He does not notice and goes on.*)
The dust ploughed into the ground.
Now let playboy Paris say
That the joy was worth the pain.

CHORUS

May you continue happy, O herald.

HERALD

I *am* happy now. Now I could die and count myself blessed.
(*a slight murmur from the Chorus*)

LEADER

This because you missed home so much.

HERALD

When you gave me that welcome, I could hardly hold my tears.

LEADER

Homesickness is a pleasant pain.

HERALD

I don't understand.

LEADER

Because you know that those whom you miss also miss you.

HERALD

Yes, that is good. Then you remembered us, eh?

LEADER

Remembered you? Black fear was on our hearts while you were away.

HERALD

Fear? Of what?

LEADER

Of that which, as you said, made us think that death might be a blessing.
(*Chorus Member shakes his head in warning*)
But of that no more. Better to keep silent now.

HERALD

Well, it's come to a happy end.
There were times when we doubted that anything would come out right again,
But up-and-down is the law, except for the gods.
You back home can't have any idea.
If it was rotten, dirty, miserable, we got it.
Imagine the stink of a ship packed to the gunwales with men,
Under a blistering sky—
And when we got ashore, we wished we were back being seasick:
The fool officers always picked our campsite
Just within range of a good Trojan bow;
And after a day of fighting or standing around
We'd fall down to sleep in the sopping grass
Until our clothes smelled like bad cheese and the harness rotted.
And if you find a few Trojan lice in your clothes tonight
You can thank me for them.
Oh, and the winter: you think it's cold in Greece?
This was unbelievable.
Every time a wind would blow off Mount Ida

Birds would fall from the air as if they'd been struck by
a slingstone.
But why go on? It's all over now—
All over for the dead; they're out of harm's way;
And we won't worry about them: sometimes we even called
them lucky.
(*Clytemnestra enters quietly*)
But now we're all of us lucky: lucky as Agamemnon,
And he rides higher in fortune than any man ever rode.
And soon we'll stand in bright morning in the temple square
And watch them nail the spoils to the temple walls,
And write on the walls: "This to the gods, in payment,
From the men of Argos who broke the spear of Troy."

CHORUS MEMBER

Now I know it was true, and not a dream.
I am not too old to change with newborn knowledge.

LEADER

Then let us tell the queen
This news that has made us young again.

CLYTEMNESTRA

Why tell me? My dancing time is done.
Some hours ago the fire-god hurled the news at my heart.
Since then, this square has been in shadow
While toothless old mumblers pronounced on the lightness
of my mind.
Others, who were faithful to me, kept the fires I commanded
Fed with ox-fat and sweet-scented herbs,
But here, I see, this is not done.
(*The Leader attempts to speak*)
There is nothing I wish to hear from you.
I say my dance is danced:
No. It will not begin
Until my lord is safely inside that house.
Herald, go swiftly to the shore:
Say to the Captain-General his city awaits him;

Say that a watchdog waits him in his house—
(*The Herald registers incomprehension*)
And that is his wife, who will love him as he has never been loved.
Say my heart has forgotten nothing
Since he took sail, and left his seal on me;
And as for taking pleasure with another man—
I could as easily dye metal scarlet.
(*She exits*)

HERALD

She speaks like a lady, there's no doubting it.

LEADER

We are glad you understand.
But tell us one thing, herald, before you take your message:
How is it with Menelaus?

HERALD

I would like to tell you a happy lie.

CHORUS

There are no happy lies. We know when we are prepared or when we are not prepared, one or the other.

HERALD

His ship is missing.

CHORUS

Ah—

LEADER

You spoke of a storm-wind. Was it that—

HERALD

Enough; your first arrow hit the mark.

CHORUS

Does no man know of his fate?

HERALD

Only the sun on the waves.

CHORUS

It seems the gods were angered.

HERALD

I came here to tell of victory.
Why do you make me end with all this woe?
Yes, it *would* seem the gods were angered,
For fire and sea conspired against us,
And many men whose eyes were bent on home
Are eyeless now in the cavern of fishes
And their ships broken; driftwood on nameless shores.
Our own ship rode the storm, but Menelaus'
Is gone out of sight.
But let me end with good words. If he is alive
He may be grieving for *us*, as we for him,
And he will soon come home in the happy sunlight,
To the smiling god—
Let me speak good—there may be hope—

(*His words choke him. He runs out.*)

CHORUS

A child's name
May carry a shadow,
A hint in sound
If named too well:
What god stood by
At the birth of Helen
To name that beauty
The bride of Hell?

She smiled while borne
From her great lord's chamber,
A smile uncaring
For all men's tears;
And over the sea
There followed after
A thousand ships
And a forest of spears.

She walked great Troy;
Her smile was changeless;

They lit bright torches
And cried her name,
Till the bridal song
Was turned to screaming;
The laughing dancers
Were bathed in flame.

So with the man
Who stole from a lion
And bore to his house
Its small soft young:
It rolled in play
Like a harmless kitten
And licked the hand
With its tiny tongue.

But the beast waxed strong
And its name was Lion,
With blood its hunger
And death its will.
It walked the house
Like a thing of terror,
Too cunning to capture,
Too great to kill.

Was Helen sent
To bring down Fortune
And spill the blood
Made hot with Pride?

(*The sound of the approaching host begins to be heard*)

Have we not seen
The end of evil?
Will many die
As many died?

(*The host begins to enter. With Agamemnon in his chariot, drawn by four Trojans of noble rank, is Cassandra.*)

CHORUS

Eternal glory
By Zeus all-seeing
Now to our king
Be freely given;
And may swift Justice
Steer to fulfillment
All things moving
In earth and heaven.

Great Agamemnon!

LEADER

O my dear lord, I would wish no better thing
Than for you to believe my joy at seeing you
My own like the voice of breath or beat of blood.
I will not give you false, twisted smiles
And lick the floor with praises of your mighty deeds,
But speak fairly and frankly.
My thoughts were against you in the beginning,
When your glorious words lashed so many of our young men
To rush unthinking to the hungry grave
For the honor of one wild young girl.
But the end is good, as your messenger said,
And thereby approves the means.
You have succeeded, and we love you.
Ask about the city; you shall find
We have been true, though others have not.

AGAMEMNON

First I hail Argos and her gods,
Who know the right cause from the wrong
And brought us safe to shelter, while their wrath
Sent Justice, through our arms, to break great Troy.
Through them I have triumphed, and let them now see
That I do not forget a debt.
We were executors of no human judgment;
The gods themselves withdrew mercy

From the proud dog Priam and his lax race.
They are no more.
We were right, and therefore ruthless.
We fell like a lion on their towered city:
The smoke of her burning still goes up,
Carrying perfumed lust and painted glory
In a storm of ashes.
Now the gods are thanked, and I turn to you.
For what you said—remember those last phrases.
I know how false a friend can be—
A shadow in a glass, a whispering specter—
When envy of another's fortune strikes the heart.
Only one man was not a backstabber,
A malcontent, a frustrator of my plans,
And that was Ulysses, who at the beginning
Was least eager of all those mouthing warhawks
To follow my spear to Troy. This to his credit, wherever
  he may be.
I am of a great mind now to call the Council
And begin the reordering of the state, which it
  doubtless needs.
I can see from the joy that greeted me that cancers
  have grown
That need the gentle knife and white-hot iron.
I go now to my home, my true seat, the palace of my fathers,
And for this victory, may our name live forever.
(*Enter Clytemnestra*)

CLYTEMNESTRA

You will all forgive me, I know, if I seem immodest
In looking such love at the man who owns my heart,
But it has been a long time, and I am not good at pretending.
What can a woman do? The world of men
Is more important to them than her love.
But I am not thinking of "men" and "women";
I am thinking of what went on in my own heart
While this man was away.

I am thinking of all the tears I shed,
Of nights black with fear and days gray with terror.
Did you know how many times, when messengers came
saying
That your bones lay in the ground by the walls of Troy,
I hanged myself, and was cut down by frightened slaves, and
went on living,
Till I ran out of tears and my heart dried up
Do you know what it is like, in a city without a king?
Prowling cutthroats, desperate men,
Troublemakers, subverters of the state,
Come out like bone-crunching hyenas at night;
And only one lonely woman to stave them off.
It is for that reason that your son
Does not stand by me to welcome his father.
I have put Orestes in safe hands;
An old comrade of yours, Strophius, has taken him far away,
Clear of this anarchic nightmare, Argos.
But now! Why, now all is changed: the king is back;
Sun shines once more; the earth drinks in your majesty
like rain;
The very pillars of our house, this aged tower,
Stand tall for confidence.
Come, dear my love,
Enter and claim the reward you so richly deserve.
Yet stay!
It is not meet that one whose foot
Was sanctified by God to crush high Troy
Should walk on this foul courtyard.
Maidens! Slaves!
Let a path of crimson spring up into the house
That our high king may walk where Justice leads him,
To a welcome that he never thought to see.
(Clytemnestra's handmaidens spread a carpet of purple stuffs from the chariot to the palace door)

AGAMEMNON

This farce has gone far enough.
I am thoroughly persuaded that you missed me—
You said so in a speech almost as long as my absence—
But to treat me as some damned Persian
Who sucks up flattery and sits limp-wristed on a
godlike throne
Is something I will not bear.
I am a soldier, and if you give me a general's honors,
I will take them;
I am a king, and it is my place to command and to be obeyed;
But I am a man, and I can walk on the ground as other men do.
To soil these beautiful things with my boots,
To grind them into the dirt, to waste them,
for my own glory—
Why, that is as if I sacrificed to *myself*,
My own god and my own priest,
And that is arrogant, blasphemous madness, that is spitting
in the face of true gods, that is mocking the divine
order and daring it to revenge itself;
And, make no mistake, *it will.*

CLYTEMNESTRA

Does all this mean you are afraid?

AGAMEMNON

I meant exactly what I said.

CLYTEMNESTRA

If *Priam* had won, would *he* have acted as if he were
ashamed of his greatness?

AGAMEMNON

Priam? He would have trod on the purple without a thought.
Perhaps that is why he did not win.

CLYTEMNESTRA

Of course, if what people will say is troubling you—

AGAMEMNON

Do they need to say it? Look at their faces.

CLYTEMNESTRA

Envy! The envy of meanness is always the measure
of greatness!

AGAMEMNON

Is this the woman I remember?
Can this be a woman still?

CLYTEMNESTRA

I *had* thought that if you loved me you would desire to
please me;
But no one makes up Agamemnon's mind but Agamemnon
himself.
(*pause*)

AGAMEMNON

Take off my boots.
(*The boots are removed. He still hesitates.*)
And how do we know who is watching from the sky
As I crush these fair things into the courtyard's filth?

CLYTEMNESTRA

This is not a pauper's house, O King.
There is Tyrian purple in the royal stores
Enough to carpet Argos with these footcloths,
And the great sea will serve when that runs dry.
I would have walked this path a thousand times
If such had been the price of your return.
(*pause*)

AGAMEMNON

The girl Cassandra should be looked after kindly.
It is not her fault that she has been made a slave.
(*He enters the palace*)

CLYTEMNESTRA

God, God, you who bring all things to pass,
You know my prayers. Now let them be fulfilled.
(*She follows him. The rest of the host exits.*)

CHORUS

Why should I fear? The city lies

Under my master's hand;
The keel that ploughed the waves to Troy
Lies beached in Argos' sand;

But one has yet to reach the shore,
And fangs of rock still wait
That ship which sails uncharted waves:
Great Agamemnon's fate.

No siren's song, no sybil's speech,
Not all of wit and worth
Can charm back home the innocent blood
That soaks the innocent earth.

One chamber of the human heart
Holds pride and strength within,
The next, a mad, sick animal,
And the wall between is thin.

Yet still I track some slippery hope
Among my icy fears,
Angling for a phantom fish
In a lake of tears.

(*Clytemnestra re-enters*)

CLYTEMNESTRA

You, girl—Cassandra or whatever your name is:
We have work for you within.
You may bear a warm bowl of scented water.
Did you hear me, you proud slut?
Thank the gods you were sent to a house old in power
and wealth,
And not to some new-rich upstart who would thrash you as
someone once thrashed him.

LEADER

Perhaps she speaks a language strange as the crying
of swallows
And cannot understand.

CLYTEMNESTRA

She had better understand.

LEADER

Cassandra, if you know what is being said to you, we beg
of you, obey.
You will only be forced to, later.

CLYTEMNESTRA

Oh, she knows what I am saying, well enough.
I fancy she spoke excellent Greek in Agamemnon's tent.
Very well, then, stay. If you like that chariot so much
We will have you chained in it until you rot.
I waste no more time. There are greater things
to be seen to.
(*She goes back into the palace*)

LEADER

Come, Cassandra. We do not hate you.
Yield now to Necessity. Better bow than break.

CASSANDRA

God! God! God!

LEADER

She is mad, or the handmaiden of the god.

CHORUS MEMBER

Or we are mad, or all the world is mad.
(*Cassandra comes down from the chariot*)

CASSANDRA

Apollo, my trust, have you brought me to ruin?
What is this house? Who is the king here?

LEADER

This is the house of Atreus.

CHORUS MEMBER

The home of Agamemnon, your master.

CASSANDRA

This is the house of Hell.
This is the winepress of death. Are you not all drowning
in blood?

(*She points at the altar*)
The flesh of the children is roasted, that their father
will be fed.
Do you hear their cry?

CHORUS MEMBER

We have had enough of evil speech in this courtyard.
(*pointing toward the seashore*)
If you must prophesy, prophesy to the waves.

LEADER

Wait. What does she see?

CASSANDRA

I see that doom is certain,
For gray and stinking, from their caves beneath the earth,
The Furies have come, and huddle like bats about this
god-hated house,
Eating into the brain with their high unbearable song.

LEADER

What this is I do not understand,
But it is black horror.

CASSANDRA

Red, red!
She has lain with him in love, and now that hand,
That hand caressing, feels for the cold hilt—no, no!
Draw the water, cast the net;
You are fishing for doom. Gather here, dark ones;
Your prey is walking within;
The great beast is going to the water
And the sting of death.

CHORUS MEMBER

O gods, what do you call down upon this house?
(*The Leader restrains him*)

CASSANDRA

Now I will sing my own doom,
Not for the ears of men but for Apollo who loved me,
Whose body touched mine by Scamander Water,

And whose breath mixed with mine.
You have set me upon a hard path, Apollo.
Now no more will I drink at the stream of my fathers,
Or walk the white city in the morning light;
For he whose foot ground out the flame of Troy
Will soon go down to darkness, and his strength,
My last help, shall be gone,
And I will be the bride of cold iron
And queen forever in a land of soundless night.

LEADER

This is great sorrow. This deadly second sight is the curse of a god?

CASSANDRA

The curse? No, no; the *gift*;
It was the bride-price of great Apollo;
To possess my body he touched my eyes with light.

LEADER

And you . . . ?

CASSANDRA

I swore to yield myself;
But I was of no mind to enter such a dreadful dynasty
By bearing a god's child. When the time came I refused.

LEADER

But the gift of prophecy was given,
And a god cannot withdraw his word.

CASSANDRA

Oh, this was seen to. When I told the truth, I never was believed.

LEADER

We believe you. Though from a far country
You know of the Feast of Thyestes, a thing
That is spoken of in whispers even here.
(*The spell seizes her again*)
The holy evil is upon her.
May some god pity her agony.

CHORUS MEMBER

What monstrous thing will we be made to see now?

CASSANDRA

The children! The children!
I hear their cry! I see them!
The generations go down in blood;
Doom walks in fire, Time is a falling mountain;
The innocent begets the cold-eyed jackal;
The all-destroying lion falls;
His mate becomes the jackal's bitch,
And both together lap the lion's blood.
That great golden beast, stiff and fly-blown on a
marble floor,
How could he know? She is no woman, nor any animal,
But a monster, a spawn of hell, chaos, not nature.
Her eyes turn toward me!
I see my doom now like a moving flame!
Agamemnon! Dead!

LEADER

You have said enough.

CASSANDRA

I have not said anything, if you have not understood.

LEADER

We pray that such a thing may never happen.

CASSANDRA

Yes, pray. Pray while *they* act.
(*She removes her crown of fillets and casts it
and her staff to earth*)
There, Apollo, take them back;
Make some other woman miserable with your kindness.
We two are done. You have turned everyone I loved against me,
But that does not matter because they are all dead now
Under the broken walls of Troy.
Having starved and lived in ditches,
I am no longer as beautiful as when you sought me

By Scamander Water, but it is all the same.
I have seen an altar-stone swilled with my father's blood,
And mine will soon be shed.
I only pray the stroke will be quick
And the pain not too great.
(*She looks at the Chorus*)
I need friends.

CHORUS MEMBER

Is there no way you can escape?

CASSANDRA

Not when the day is here.
Now indeed I can cry my prophecies to the waves;
But of darker waters than the ones you meant.

LEADER

You are a brave woman. You will be remembered.

CASSANDRA

I remember those who were brave: my father and brothers.
I must be brave for them.
(*She moves toward the palace, but turns at the door*)
I am going in now.
Do not weep. I die in royal company,
And I shall be avenged.
Sun, I see you for the last time:
Guide with your light that wandering man;
For when at last he comes again to Argos
And passes through these doors, his bright sword drawn,
That day shall Agamemnon's mighty ghost
And the small shade of one forgotten girl
Lie down to rest forever.
Poor Humankind. Your happiness ends with the fall of a shadow
But your misery only with eternal night.
And to know this—that is the worst of all.
(*She enters the palace*)

CHORUS

No man is wise who cannot say to Fortune,

"Enough from your golden hands,"
For he sees himself the master of all around him
And famous in many lands;

He strides like a walking tower in the sun of glory
And all bow down before;
And then one day, enthroned in pride and greatness,
He hears a closing door.

He is all alone, in his mouth the taste of ashes
That he knows for the sum of his life;
And the only light, as he sits in the hollow darkness,
Is the gleaming edge of a knife.

(*Agamemnon screams within*)

LEADER

It is done.
What shall we do?

CHORUS

Raise a hue and cry. Get the townspeople to back us.
Then we can act.

No. Burst in on them now. Take them with their butcher-work
still red on their hands.

I think that may be the best thing. This is a situation
that calls for immediate action.

He's right. No time to waste—It's clear they mean to
set up a tyranny.

We must act now. We can't let them trample down our
rights.

Better death than submission.
But first we must be sure we're doing the right thing.

That's true. Mere good intentions won't bring back the dead.

Besides, how do we know the king *is* dead?
Hearing a scream proves nothing.

CHORUS MEMBER

Let us get the facts straight.
Then our rage can burst forth.
(*Enter Clytemnestra, her hands and dress stained with blood*)

CLYTEMNESTRA

I spoke so many empty words,
Words of love, and my heart a cinder of hate.
Now I throw them all to the ground
And think no shame on it.
My smooth words wove a snare that caught and held;
My lies built a circle of sharp stakes
That even that great beast could not leap over.
The gods know how long this was in coming—
How many times he earned his due.
Helpless and naked in his bath, I cast the
rich robes about him,
Netted him, held him fast,
And pushed a blade of iron through the silk.
Twice I drove it home, and he screamed like a beast
And that great purple sack pitched and buckled to the floor.
They say the third time is the charm, so I brought down
the edge
And the air squelched from him, and a fountain of
bright blood
Shot up and fell on me like the sweet rain on the
young shoots in spring.
Now you know, and may it make you happy.
For me, I glory. This man filled our cup
With pain unspeakable;
Now he is home, and has drunk it to the dregs.

LEADER

You glory in it—and this man was your own lord.

CLYTEMNESTRA

Yes, that man was my husband . . . Agamemnon.

Now he is dead, and this hand, this good workman, did it.
That is all that makes any difference.
What you think of it means nothing to me.

CHORUS

Whether you did this coldly
Or whether some poisonous herb worked your brain
to madness,
In those three strokes you cut yourself away
From humankind, from love, from rest on this earth.

CLYTEMNESTRA

You judge me? You threaten me with exile?
You should have said those words to this dead dog
When his yellow-toothed priests tore the throat from
the lamb of my womb
To charm the winds of Thrace.
You should have hunted *him* from this land
With stones and curses, as you would use me now.
Very well, then. If you can make good your threats, so be it,
But if the power falls to me, be assured
You shall learn wisdom, late
Though it is for you to learn.

CHORUS

You will remember this some day:
Some day, when there is no appeal.

CLYTEMNESTRA

For that, I swear to you
By the crying of my child's blood, that now is stilled,
And by the dark goddess of Hell, to whom I now consign
Agamemnon's ghost,
I shall fear nothing while the presence of Aegisthus
Warms this house like a fire, and stands between me
and danger like a rock.
As for this other, he lies as was his custom,
Bedded with a gilded whore of Troy,
Though this a prophetess, her legs spread on the marble

As on the rough planks of her late lord's ship,
Her swan song dead upon her lying lips.
There let them lie. Their memory will give
A sharper pleasure to my bed's delight.

CHORUS

So it has come to undying fame:
The flower of blood that is Helen's name.
Great cold, great sleep
Cover our town.
The strong tower is fallen,
The great shield is down.

CLYTEMNESTRA

A double waste of old men's breath:
To curse Helen, and pray for death.

CHORUS

Who will weep for you now, O King?
And who to the grave your bones will bring?
Great cold, great sleep
Cover our town.
The strong tower is fallen,
The great shield is down.

CLYTEMNESTRA

Let the daughter he murdered greet him with tears,
For I have had none, these many years.

CHORUS

The spider-queen has stung your life,
But the curse of Atreus drove the knife.
Great cold, great sleep
Cover our town.
The strong tower is fallen,
The great shield is down.

CLYTEMNESTRA

Then never the hand of queen or wife,
But the hand of Justice, drove the knife.

CHORUS

(*to Clytemnestra*)

That blood on your breast will be fresh one day,
And death for death will another repay.
Great cold, great sleep
Cover our town.
The strong tower is fallen,
The great shield is down.

CLYTEMNESTRA

Listen to me. I ask no more than this:
The knowledge that I have set the balance straight,
Wiped clean the print of blood, and laid to rest
The doom that has walked this house so many years.

CHORUS

Who can decide this thing? And who
Can wash off blood with blood?
I only know, as one does,
To him shall it be done,
And so following,
World without end.

(*Enter Aegisthus with his bodyguard*)

AEGISTHUS

So: the bright day of Justice, and at last
I can begin to feel there is a God,
Watching this dead beast tangled in the purple
Paying in full for the tricks his father contrived.
Do you know that story, Argives? It is time
The tale of the Feast of Thyestes was cried to the clouds.
Atreus, this man's father, drove his own brother from the land—
My father, Thyestes—in a dispute about the throne.
Then, when Thyestes came in misery after long years
A suppliant to his hearth, Agamemnon's father
Smiled his dog's smile, and invited him
To a feast of reconciliation, roast meat and wine.
But the meat that was served that day

Was Thyestes' own children, and when that royal jester
Showed Thyestes the heads of the game he had eaten
He leaped up, and vomited the meat from his mouth,
And kicking over the laden table, cried,
"May the gods do this to the whole house of Atreus."
Then was he driven into banishment again
To share with me, his third-born,
Those years of voiceless, impotent sorrow.
But now I have found a voice, and an arm,
And now I have come home.
I planned this deed, and if I die, I die.
The slate is clean.

CHORUS

Nothing is clean, Aegisthus. The slate is sticky
with blood.
You have added blood-guilt to blood-guilt, and piled it on
your own head.

AEGISTHUS

I am going to tell you something, old men:
Don't meddle in royal matters.
It serves little for the galley-slaves to spit
At the ship's master on the deck above.
Not while there are whips, and chains, and hunger's
iron tooth.
Is my meaning clear?

CHORUS

So you have found an arm, you coward:
Yes, a *woman's* arm.

AEGISTHUS

Why, naturally. Should I have come to Argos
With "I am here to kill Agamemnon" written above my heart?
My motives for hatred were too well known.
No, the deception was the woman's part,
And well has she done her work.

CHORUS

O god of the sun, make Orestes tall and strong
And light his way home to vengeance on these two.

AEGISTHUS

You have howled enough. Disperse now,
Before I have my men whip you to your kennels.

CHORUS

Men of Agamemnon! Soldiers of Argos! Help us!

AEGISTHUS

The soldiers of Argos will follow the man who pays them,
And pay them I shall, with Agamemnon's gold.

LEADER

Let every man take up stock and stone.

AEGISTHUS

Guards! They threaten us. Let your swords do their work.

CHORUS

To the death, then, usurper! The gods judge between us!
(*Clytemnestra comes between them*)

CLYTEMNESTRA

No more, my dearest. We have seen a bitter harvest-time,
A letting of foul blood from ancient sins.
Now let the grass grow over the torn earth,
The scarred flesh heal.
Let us all learn to say "Enough."
Old men of Argos, you have sustained your honor;
Go to your homes before you meet with harm.
What was done, we had to do,
And what is done, is done.

CHORUS

You think this tale of blood is finished?
It has not yet begun.

AEGISTHUS

Listen to that. Treasonous old fools,
I am your king,

And I will not forget this day.

CHORUS

If you do forget, you will be reminded when Orestes
comes home.

AEGISTHUS

Exiles are eaters of wind and empty dreams.
I was one long enough. I know.

CHORUS

You have turned a royal palace to a slaughterhouse and
an honored kingdom to a dunghill.
Now crow over it, like a cock with his hen.

CLYTEMNESTRA

Dogs bark loudest that cannot bite.
Forget them, dearest. We hold the power,
And you and I shall order all things well.

(*They go into the palace*)

ACT II

The Libation Bearers

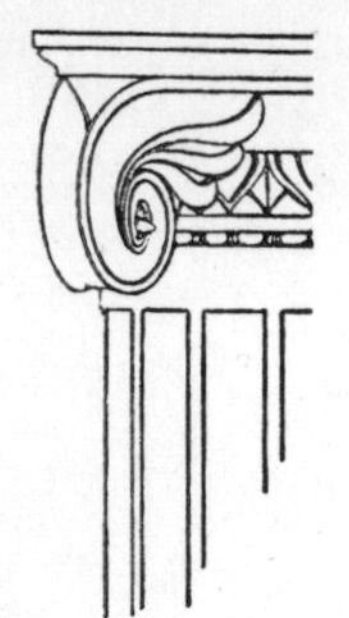

Characters

ORESTES
PYLADES
ELECTRA
SERVANT
CLYTEMNESTRA
CILISSA
AEGISTHUS
CHORUS OF MAIDSERVANTS

Scenes

Argos. The tomb of Agamemnon; the palace. Some years have passed.

(*The tomb of Agamemnon. Enter Orestes and Pylades.*)

ORESTES

Hermes, lord of the dead,
Be with me now. I stand by the grave of my father,
On the soil I called home.
(*He lays a lock of hair on the tomb*)
Hear me, Father. I leave this lock of hair,
An offering of manhood and of grief.
I was not here when they struck you down,
Not here to stretch out my hand as they carried your corpse
to this tomb.
(*A procession of women approaches*)
What does this mean? Has death come again to our house?
Or does someone still remember my father?
O God, that girl—it must be—
Pylades, look—my sister—Electra.
Come, out of the way.
(*They conceal themselves*)

CHORUS

I come from a house of blood
With blood upon my breast,
For as my nails have torn my flesh
Foul dreams have torn my rest.

Last night one cried in the dark
The scream of a horrible birth:
She had borne a dream of the restless dead
And the fires beneath the earth.

I am sent to bribe the dead
From that palace that all men shun

By the godless woman who rules the house
That never sees the sun.

The glory of old is gone
With the loveliness of light;
High Fortune capers and dances there
On the terrible edge of night.

There Murder walks with Lust,
And where their fingers stray
Not all the waters of all the earth
Can wash the blood away.

Meanwhile, I serve them both
And close a silent gate
On bitter tongue and raging heart,
Sorrow, and secret hate.

ELECTRA

You women, maidservants of the house of Atreus,
Tell me what to say.
Give me the words to pour out with these libations
On my father's grave.
Should I say "I pour out the love and tears of a
faithful wife"—
And mean my mother?
Or is this better: "Reward the givers of these sweet offerings
For their gift of—a filthy crime?"
Or should I just spill them out, dumb and dishonored,
the way my father died,
With my face turned away as if I were emptying slops?
Tell me, please. I truly don't know.
Don't be afraid. Remember we're sisters in hatred.
Remember the hour strikes for the free man
As well as for the slave.

CHORUS

Because I respect your father's grave as I respect the holy places,
I will tell you my thoughts.

ELECTRA

Speak them.

CHORUS

As you pour, pronounce blessings on those of good will.

ELECTRA

Who do I have to call friend?

CHORUS

Yourself first; then all of those who hate Aegisthus.

ELECTRA

Shall I include you then?

CHORUS

The naming of names is for you to decide.

ELECTRA

Who stands with us in this?

CHORUS

Though he's far away, remember Orestes.

ELECTRA

Thank you. I shall not forget.

CHORUS

Then the murderers. Pray against them—

ELECTRA

Yes. Tell me. Give me the words.

CHORUS

That there may come a man, or more than man . . .

ELECTRA

To judge, or to punish?

CHORUS

To take blood for blood. Say only that.

ELECTRA

Is this a seemly prayer in the eyes of the gods?

CHORUS

You have been struck. Is it impious to wish to strike back?

ELECTRA

Hermes, lord of the dead,
Be with me now. I stand by the grave of my father.
Father, hear me. I say this prayer for myself and for
your son Orestes.
Our mother made us slaves and homeless wanderers;
She traded us for Aegisthus, the man who planned your murder.
O Father, let Orestes come back home.
Let me see him again.
And let me never be like my mother.
For our enemies, let them be killed as they killed you.
This is my prayer.

CHORUS

Between good and evil,
Stand beside this mound:
Here, where the tear falls
And breaks on the ground
As our king was broken,
Make a solemn sound.

Hear us from your darkness;
Hear and befriend.
Strong bow, sharp sword
Let the just gods send
To this house of terror:
Come, and make an end.

ELECTRA

Women, look here.

CHORUS

What is it?

ELECTRA

Here, by the tomb—a lock of hair.

CHORUS

What man's? Or is it a girl's?

ELECTRA

No one would have done this but myself.

CHORUS

Yes, the ones who *should* do these things are eaten up
with hate.

ELECTRA

It isn't mine—and yet it's so very *like* mine . . .

CHORUS

Orestes?

ELECTRA

I don't know—what else to think.

CHORUS

Then he—

ELECTRA

No. He might have cut it and sent it by some stranger.

CHORUS

Perhaps. And all the sadder if it's true. It means he'll
never set foot upon this land again.

ELECTRA

To think of that is like a sword in my heart.
Is *this* the answer to my prayer?
No—if I start to cry I'll never stop.
O God, how could I believe this lock came from the head of
a common man?
My mother? No. Expect a sweet act of grief from one who
no longer even belongs to nature?
And yet—how can I be sure it comes from that most
loved of men?
If only it could speak, could whisper a word
To stop this tearing and twisting of my heart, to tell me
Whether to throw it away like a hated thing
Or to water it with a fellow-mourner's tears
And replace it proudly on our father's grave.

CHORUS

We call upon the gods, who know
How the wingèd seed of hope is tossed by the storm;

And yet, if it chance to fall on fertile ground,
How mighty a tree may rise up from that place.
(*Orestes appears from his hiding place*)

ORESTES

Thank the gods. They have answered half your prayer.
Now pray for the rest.

ELECTRA

What do I have, that I should thank the gods for it?

ORESTES

What you sought.

ELECTRA

How do you know what was in my heart?

ORESTES

I know that, among other things, Orestes was there.

ELECTRA

Then how is half my prayer answered?

ORESTES

You prayed to see him. Look before you.

ELECTRA

Is this a trap?

ORESTES

If it is, I am the one who's caught in it.

ELECTRA

You overheard me. You're making fun of me.

ORESTES

Look in my eyes, if you think I'm laughing.

ELECTRA

But—how can I be sure—

ORESTES

You saw only a lock of hair,
And it was as if I stood before you.
Now here I am, and you won't believe it.
Look. Here is the place the lock was cut from.
Is it still the gift of a stranger?

Look at this sash.
Your hands were smaller when you wove the cloth
With its design of running beasts.
(*She starts to cry out*)
No, no, dearest, keep hold of yourself:
We are too close to those who hate us
To lose our heads for joy.

ELECTRA

O my own, my four-times beloved,
Because you have come to stand in our father's place,
And because the love that I would have borne our mother
goes to you,
And my love for our sister, sacrificed at Aulis,
And because you of all men have come to stand up for me
And bring us to our own.
Trust now to your strength, and let Might and Right
And Zeus, the great third, stand beside you.

ORESTES

Zeus. Zeus. Hear these grave words, and guide what
we must do.
You see here the children of the eagle
Stricken down by the deadly snake.
The nest is deserted, and the young ones perish.
Save them, O Zeus. It is myself I mean,
And my sister Electra,
Homeless the one and helpless the other.
Sustain us, O Zeus. If you leave us naked to the winds,
The children of a father who honored you so greatly,
What will become of the faith of men?
The stump of this royal tree can still serve as your altar,
But not if you let it be blasted to the ground.
Cherish it, and a shoot may still spring to immortal glory,
Though now it seem dry and low.

CHORUS

Children, children, saviors of your father's house and honor,

No more of that. Idle ears may hear,
And busy tongues carry your thoughts to those who hold
the power,
Those whom I long to see
Stiff on the pitch-pine pyre,
Black in the heart of the flame.

ORESTES

Apollo holds the power, and he will not forsake me.
His oracle told me to stake all on this chance:
"Give them a taste of their own," he said,
"Come down upon them like a blood-crazed bull."
If I did not, he promised nothing but horror.
The undone deed would come out upon me
In cancer, in rotting sores: my flesh would die alive;
Or the dark ones would haunt me, the Furies that eat
the brain.
He spoke of the sudden terror in the dead hour,
The monstrous shadow approaching the bed;
Told how a man may be driven from city to city, from
road to road,
Sharing no cup of friendship in a welcoming house,
Turned back from holy altars by a father's curse,
Until at last in some ditch, gnawed by cold and wretchedness,
He finds his only friend, Death.
Should I believe such an oracle? What difference
does it make,
When even if I do not, the thing must still be done?
I have motives enough to drive me on:
The will of the gods, the giant grief of my father,
Myself driven from my estates, and the people of Argos,
My people, that wrestled down the might of Troy,
Slaves to a brace of women: for Aegisthus is woman-hearted,
Or, if he is not, he can prove it soon in my face.

CHORUS

Great Zeus, we pray that your thunder-stone

Be dashed in the teeth of those grinning mouths
Dripping with venom of hate;
That the great wheel be turned again,
Blood-greased, groaning with the voice of living men,
That tells the cycles of fate.

ORESTES

Father, how can I reach down through the darkness?
What word, what act can throw a gleam
Into your stone-sealed night?
From my eyes should fall fire, not sickly tears,
Remembering the greatness of your days,
The roaring blood, the light.

CHORUS

Child, the red teeth of the flame
Eat only the body of the dead;
His will is a stubborn stone,
White-hot; but touch it with a tear,
The stone will break, the ghost will rise,
Dreadful, to claim his own.

ELECTRA

Father, Father, hear us! Hear our cry!
We have only your low grave to shelter us
Against the black wind,
Against the iron night.
Before the monstrous darkness fall,
Tall-plumed, terrible in arms,
Rise! Rise into the light!

ORESTES

If you had died in the storming of burning Troy,
Your great heart split by a bronze-tipped spear
Or under a falling tower,
You would lie today in a cairn like a mighty mountain,
Your dead face covered by a mask of gold
With a smile of immortal power.

CHORUS

And Agamemnon's giant ghost,
Among the great companions, the Argive heroes,
Would move to his place of pride
As a great star walks in fire among lesser stars
Through the country of night, to a royal throne
By death-lord Hermes' side.

ELECTRA

No! No! I wish he had never died!
Not by the side of blood-churned Scamander
With the broken yield of the spear;
But that those who wished him evil were dead
By some nightmare means, in distant lands
Whispered in silent fear.

CHORUS

Child, you are spending the gold of dreams.
The north wind blows vain wishes away
And scatters them far and wide.
But the lash that shall punish those of bloody hand
Screams over their heads in the darkened air:
The gods have taken your side.

ORESTES

Ah, this agony pierces me like a sword!
So let my cry speed like a singing arrow
To sting these powers awake!
Zeus, Zeus, let some great stone-eyed creature rise
up from the ground
To crush those two into dust.

CHORUS

I claim the right to sing my savage joy
About the pyre where their corpses burn.
I have bitten my lips too long
Against the indignation of my heart,
Whipped by anger as the prow by the howling salt-blast.

ELECTRA

Aie! Zeus, smash their skulls with your fist!
Hear me, Earth! Hear me, you gods of darkness!

CHORUS

Blood cries for blood. The seed of the second death
Is sown in the stroke of the first.
See it done, you Furies. Give us a sign.

ORESTES

You Curses that wander the land beneath the earth,
Powers of the kingdom of death, give us a sign.
We are the last of the house of Atreus
And we have nothing. O God, where shall we turn?

ELECTRA

We have one thing: our mother's inheritance—
The gift of the wolf, a savage implacable heart—
She who without a tear shoveled our father into the ground.

CHORUS

Ah, that day I clawed at my streaming cheeks;
I battered my head and breast and wailed the high deathsong
to the skies.

ORESTES

I ask this of the gods:
Let me live long enough to kill her.

CHORUS

Listen: to cripple the strong hand of your father's ghost
They chopped the corpse's hands from its body.

ELECTRA

Ah! And while they were butchering you, Father,
They flung me into a room and locked the door
As if I were a mad dog, and left me to drown in my tears.
Hear this, Father. Listen to these words.

CHORUS

Let these words burn deep.
Let them eat into the quiet soul.

Only so will the rage of blood awaken.
Pray for that time so long delayed,
And let your will, when you have prayed,
Have the simplicity of fire or stone.

ORESTES

O Zeus, give me my kingdom.

ELECTRA

O Persephone, let me see Aegisthus die.

ORESTES

O Earth, when I face those two
Let my father come forth to see!

CHORUS

My flesh crawls to hear their prayer.
Let it come, let it come, this dreadful thing they ask,
For the blood thickens with cold; the heart of this house
Is numb with ingrown pain,
The agony not to be borne, the worm that eats all away.

ELECTRA

Father! Father, be with your children!

ORESTES

Remember the shame of your death!

ELECTRA

They netted you like a beast!

ORESTES

Helpless, naked, they struck you down!

ELECTRA

Does that not rouse you from your darkness, Father?

ORESTES

Will you not rear upright that beloved head?

ELECTRA

Do not let your house perish, Father.
A man's children are the voices of his blood
When he is gone from earth,
Like floats that hold the net from sinking in the deep.

Hear us, Father. Our grief and shame are yours,
And our prayers for ourselves are also prayers for you.

CHORUS

Children, you have spoken well.
Now the rest must be action.

ORESTES

It will be. But tell me first why my mother sends you
with libations.
Some hypocritical remorse?
Tell me what you know about it.

CHORUS

I know all about it, for I was there.
It was a dream she had.
That godless woman was shaken
By drifting terrors in the night.
Because of it, she sent these offerings out.

ORESTES

Can you tell me exactly what it was?

CHORUS

Yes; she told me. She dreamed she gave birth to a serpent.

ORESTES

Was there more to the dream?

CHORUS

She dressed it as if it were a baby
And when it was hungry, she gave her breast to it.

ORESTES

So that it tore her nipple with its fangs.

CHORUS

Yes, and drew in blood along with the milk.

ORESTES

This is no empty dream. This is the vision of a man.

CHORUS

She woke up screaming in the blind dark.
They had to light lamps all over the palace.

At any rate, this is why she sends these offerings to
be poured:
To free her of—whatever it was.

ORESTES

By the earth and my father's grave
I pray that this omen is meant for me.
Yes, it must be; the parts all fit.
If this snake came out of the place from which I came,
Fastened its jaws on the breast from which I drew milk
And pierced the flesh with its fangs, drawing forth blood
and savage pain,
It must mean that my mother will be murdered by the creature
she bore.
I am the snake; I am the one who will kill her.

CHORUS

You have interpreted well.
May it all happen as you have said.
Now tell your friends what they must do—
Or not do, as need be.

ORESTES

This is how it will be:
Electra will go inside,
And at all costs keep secret what has happened.
Let me make this emphatic: it must be this way
If those two are to be tricked to their doom
As they tricked a noble and open-hearted man to his.
And that is how it will happen; Apollo has said so,
And Apollo's word has never been false.
Now. My friend Pylades and myself, disguised as travelers
And talking like outlanders, go to the outer gate
And ask to see Aegisthus.
Then, once I am over that doorstone, and through those gates,
And find that man sitting on my father's throne,
The minute he rises, and looks me in the eye,
And says "Who are you?" I'll give him an answer

Swift, and sharp, and cold, through the middle of his body.
Electra, go in now, and keep your eyes open and your
lips closed.
You other women,
If you can say something that will help our plot, say it;
If not, keep quiet.
Pylades, you will second me: you and the god Apollo,
Whom I call on now to guide the work of my sword.
(*Exit Electra, Orestes, and Pylades*)

CHORUS

The earth crawls
With unnumbered terrors;
Monstrous forms
In the sea-depths lie;
The storm-wind howls,
And far in the darkness
Things like torches
Fall through the sky.

But none can measure
The heights of daring
Man's pride may scale
Till it falls to doom,
Or fathom the blind
Down-dragging darkness,
The animal power
Of the woman's womb.

Althea lit
The torch that measured
By length of burning
Her own son's life;
And Scylla, all
For a golden necklace,
Her father's charmed hair
Shore off with a knife.

But why should I tell
Of ancient treason
When near at hand
Is the bitter tale
Of the brazen-hearted
And scheming woman
Who slew the hero
In war-lord's mail?

The sword is forged
Upon Right's hard anvil
That shall lay the guilty
Low to earth,
And the son brought home
By unswerving Justice
Stands even now
At the door of his birth.

(*Before the palace. Enter Orestes and Pylades.*)

ORESTES

(*knocking at the gate*)
You there! Inside the palace!
Is there no one at home?
Can't you hear me—or has Aegisthus no respect for the laws of hospitality?

SERVANT

All right, all right.
(*opening*)
Who are you, stranger, and where from?

ORESTES

Just tell the masters of this house
That I have news for them.
Be quick about it, will you?
The darkness is coming on, and it's time for travelers to find shelter.
Send the lady of the house to the door—
Or wait; better yet the lord.

Then we can talk as man to man
Without having to stand on the usual ceremony.
(*Enter Clytemnestra*)

CLYTEMNESTRA

Friends, if you want lodging for the night you have only
to say so.
There are all the comforts you could wish for in this house—
The beds are soft, and we'll draw a bath if you'd like one—
I can take care of that.
If you have important business to discuss, of course,
That's for the man of the house to see to, and I'll call him.

ORESTES

I'm from Phocis, Madam. While I was on the road to Argos
I met a man, a stranger to me, and we fell into talk.
He told me his name was Strophius, and he said
"As long as you're going to Argos anyway, my friend,
I'd appreciate it if you'd give Orestes' parents
A message from me: tell them that he is dead.
Please don't forget. I'm sure they'll want to know.
Then they can tell you whether they want his remains
sent home
And you can bring the message back to me
On your return. Tell them, anyway,
That we've put his ashes in a nice bronze urn
And there are many people who are sorry he is dead."
That's all. I don't know if this concerns *you*, Madam,
But I think his father ought to know about it.

CLYTEMNESTRA

Stranger, you can't know the terrible news you've given.
It's like the final curse upon this house,
Like a storm stripping an old tree bare.
I tried so hard to keep him away from this swamp of death;
I hoped that some day he could come home safe,
And be happy here, and make us happy,
And now—it's all over.

ORESTES

I wish I could have brought better news
To someone as kind and hospitable as you.
But I thought it would have broken a sacred trust
Not to keep the promise I made.

CLYTEMNESTRA

And our hospitality will not be the poorer for it, believe me.
If *you* hadn't brought the news, someone else would have,
eventually.
(*to Servant*)
Take these gentlemen to a guest room
And see to it that their treatment is worthy of this house.
In the meantime I'll tell this tragic news to the master
And discuss with our many friends what we shall do.
(*Exit Clytemnestra, Orestes, Pylades, and Servant*)

CHORUS

What words from our lips can help Orestes?
Great Earth, O you who cover the high king's grave,
The prince of the black ships of war,
Let subtle Persuasion pass through your gates of darkness
To win the aid of death-lord Hermes
To guide that unpitying sword.
(*Enter Cilissa*)
But see, our wandering man is at work already
Sowing his crop of anguish, for here is Cilissa,
The old nurse of Orestes, and in tears.
Where do you go, Cilissa, and why does Misery walk with you?

CILISSA

It's that awful woman; she wants Aegisthus brought here
To meet the strangers and hear the news from *them.*
You should have seen her in front of the servants, trying to
pull a long face,
While all the time she could hardly keep from grinning
At how nicely everything's worked out for *her,*
Even if it is the last blow to this house, this terrible news;

And I'm sure it'll make *Aegisthus* happy when he hears it.
Oh, I'm so miserable!
It's been one thing after another, but never anything like *this*.
I tried to bear up under all the other things,
But to think of poor little Orestes—
You know, I worked my hands to the bone for that child;
I cared for him right after he came out of his mother,
And at night I'd have to walk the floor with him,
While he'd scream fit to wake the dead . . .
A baby hasn't got any sense; it's just like a little animal:
Poor little thing, *it* can't tell you when it's hungry or
thirsty or has to wet;
Its little insides just make up their own rules
And you have to keep guessing, and sometimes I wouldn't
guess right,
And then I'd have to wash out his little clothes—
I was nurse and laundrywoman too, and I did a good job—
I remember how I'd take him from his father's arms;
And now I have to go tell that awful man he's dead
And watch his face light up . . .
Oh, I'm so miserable!

CHORUS

Cilissa, did she say he should come alone?

CILISSA

What? How do you mean, alone?

CHORUS

I mean, did she say he should bring his bodyguard?

CILISSA

Why, as a matter of fact she did.
And she said they should all bring their weapons.

CHORUS

Cilissa, don't do it. He mustn't be alarmed.
Just tell him to come himself.
This is a case where the messenger has to correct the message
a little.

CILISSA

You sound almost happy about all this.

CHORUS

You can never tell. Zeus has ways of suddenly changing
an evil wind to a good.

CILISSA

What "good"? Orestes, the hope of this house, is dead.

CHORUS

Only a very bad prophet would be too sure of that.

CILISSA

Wait a minute. Do you know something you're not telling me?

CHORUS

Don't try to outguess the gods, Cilissa.
Just do as we ask, and leave the rest to them.

CILISSA

Well, I don't understand, but I'll do it.
I only hope it all turns out for the best.
(*She exits*)

CHORUS

Zeus, Zeus, father of the gods,
Stand up for Orestes.
You see the colt of that famous sire
Once beloved of you
Now hitched to a heavy load of sorrows.
Cut loose the traces, Zeus,
Give him his head,
And the thoroughbred's blood
Will attend to the rest.

And you, shining Apollo, lord of light,
Lord of the great and sacred shrine of Delphi:
When will the house of Atreus raise its head to the sun?
Great Hermes, sender of fair winds,
Send victory from your strong hand.
The future is darkness till you have made clear the sign,

And secrets under the night
Are secrets still in the day.

O, when may I sing for this house's unchaining
A song of hope—no longer the mourners' keening,
But of women who stand by the shore in a fair salt breeze
Singing the great ship home?

O my prince, it is nearly time, it is nearly time.
Strike home, and do not be afraid;
And if she cries "My child!" to you,
Cry back "My father!" to her.
(*Enter Aegisthus*)

AEGISTHUS

I was asked to come here.
They say that Orestes is dead.
The news gives me no satisfaction.
This house stinks of death enough.
And how do I know that this is true?
A rumor started by a nervous woman
Flares up in the air and goes out again in smoke.
What do *you* people know about it?

CHORUS

We have heard the news, but of course we are women too.
Why not go in and hear it from the man who brought it?

AEGISTHUS

Yes, I'd better. I'll soon find out whether this man was
there at the death
Or if he's just an irresponsible talebearer.
This is a thing I have to be certain of.
(*Exit Aegisthus*)

CHORUS

Zeus, Zeus, it is time now, it is time now.
The blade trembles, it edges near its target,
The quick-beating life of man.
He has gone in, our prince has gone in,

The doors are shut, there are two against him;
Apollo—
(*a scream from inside the palace*)
It is done.
One way or the other, it is decided.
(*Servant comes running out of the main gate of the palace, toward the women's wing on the far side*)

SERVANT

He's dead! My master is dead!
You there in the women's quarters! Open the door!
Someone tell Clytemnestra!
Aegisthus is dead!
Help! Someone!
(*Enter Clytemnestra*)

CLYTEMNESTRA

What is this noise? What are you shouting about?

SERVANT

The dead man is killing the living!

CLYTEMNESTRA

I understand you—O God—too well.
Someone bring me a sword, or an ax, to kill!
I am at the end of my way; the curse has found us at last.
Bring me a sword, I say! Someone, bring me a sword!
(*Enter Orestes—with drawn sword—and Pylades*)

ORESTES

You next; we've finished with the other one.

CLYTEMNESTRA

No, no! Aegisthus, my darling, my strong one, have they killed you?

ORESTES

You love him? Very well, you can share a grave with him.

CLYTEMNESTRA

Wait, my son. I held you in my arms when you were a tiny baby—

You'd go to sleep on my breast after you'd had your milk—

ORESTES

Pylades—can I let her go—do I have to kill her—

PYLADES

Orestes, let all men hate you, but not the gods.

ORESTES

(*to Clytemnestra*)
Come here.
I'm going to kill you on his body.
His. In there.
The one you thought was a better man than my father.
You should have loved my father, but all you gave him was hate.
You have made your choice. You may sleep with this one forever.

CLYTEMNESTRA

I raised you from a baby. Will you let me grow old in your company?

ORESTES

You killed my father, and now you want to come live with me?

CLYTEMNESTRA

Fate had some part in that, my dear.

ORESTES

Then Fate says that this is the day you die.

CLYTEMNESTRA

If this meant a mother's curse on you, would that make you stop and think?

ORESTES

What "mother"? You gave birth to me, and then threw me away.

CLYTEMNESTRA

I put you in the house of a friend. I don't call that throwing you away.

ORESTES

You sold me, if you prefer. That's what it amounts to.

CLYTEMNESTRA

I sold you. And what price did I get for you, then?

ORESTES

I could tell you, but it would be too filthy to say.

CLYTEMNESTRA

And what about some of the things your father did?
I don't suppose you'd care to talk about those?

ORESTES

Don't put the blame on him.
He was suffering hardships in a strange land while you were sitting here at home.

CLYTEMNESTRA

For a woman to be without her man for ten years is a hardship, child.

ORESTES

But you managed to bear it nobly, thanks to Aegisthus.

CLYTEMNESTRA

So you've condemned your own mother to death.

ORESTES

No, Mother. You have condemned yourself.

CLYTEMNESTRA

Do this thing, and my curses will follow you like hounds.

ORESTES

Let them. My father's would, if I failed to do this.

CLYTEMNESTRA

I might as well be crying to a tomb.

ORESTES

Yes. You might as well.

CLYTEMNESTRA

So you were the snake I bore and to whom I gave my breast.

ORESTES

Yes. Your nightmare was a good prophet.

Come. You did wrong, and now you pay for it.
(*Orestes and Pylades take Clytemnestra into the palace*)

CHORUS

Even this tears my heart, as I watch them pass into night.
But I cannot weep, for I see the hoped-for, the promised good:
That Orestes has not sunk down in the terrible ocean of blood,
And the eye of Agamemnon's house still opens to light.

As Justice came at the end to Priam and Priam's land,
So, after long years, to the halls of Atreus Justice returned:
Child of Zeus, the fury was hers in our prince's eyes
that burned,
And the black wind of death that followed the sword in
Orestes' hand.

Now to the cunning and might of Apollo we make our song,
Keeper of that great chasm in Parnassus' holy ground;
What is ordained on high by men upon earth is found:
The power that is of the gods will not serve evil for long.

Hail! To the light, to the gods, to the turning wheel of
the Fates,
And to Time, that will cleanse the hearth of this palace of
all that is vile,
Till its servants, once bowed with grief, can look up again,
and smile
On the new generation of men that go in peace through
its gates.
(*The doors of the palace open, revealing Orestes standing over the bodies of Aegisthus and Clytemnestra. Pylades stands beside him, holding the purple robe in which Agamemnon was entangled and slain.*)

ORESTES

Look at them well.
Here they lie, the double-headed dragon
That killed my father and usurped my house.
Not long ago they sat on their thrones in full pride;

Now they have only the love that binds them in death.
They swore to kill my father; they swore to die together:
They have fulfilled both vows.
And now, you who would look upon evil,
Behold this. This was the web which caught my father,
The robe in which she netted him for the bloody work.
Spread it out. Come, gather in a circle
And show it to that great father—not my own,
But the golden eye of the all-seeing sun.
Let him see my mother's handiwork, and witness
That I did right, when the day of reckoning comes.
Aegisthus I do not count;
He died the death adulterers die by law—
But she, who plotted this foul thing against the man
Who gave her the children she carried in her womb—
That once-sweet burden, now bearing the deathstroke's
weight—
What name will fit her? A deadly snake
Whose very will, seething and envenomed,
Rots a man's flesh even without a bite?
And this thing: when I look at it, words fail me.
The sort of thing some crossroads-haunting thief,
Some sneaking cutthroat, might devise
To throw about his victims. Gods!
Before such a woman should be called mine,
Let me be blasted, childless, from this earth.

CHORUS

I grieve for those that have gone before,
But for you that remain, I grieve yet more.

ORESTES

Did she do it or did she not? Here is the proof;
A great robe, three times pierced by Aegisthus' sword,
Faded by time, darkened by blood . . .
The last thing that touched my father when he lived . . .
(*Burying his face in the robe, he weeps*)

Our whole house . . . on and on . . .
What filthy victory is this that I have won?

CHORUS

No man can pass to his life's end
Untouched by suffering.
One grief is here, and another is coming.

ORESTES

Listen—you must know—tell me, when is this thing going
to end?
I'm afraid; I'm like a charioteer whose horses are running wild,
off the course,
Plunging on into nothingness;
Something I don't know has gotten into my heart and it's
shrieking and dancing there.
But my mind is clear . . . listen to me;
I was right to kill my mother . . . the gods hated her . . .
She was soaked with my father's blood . . .
And Apollo told me—his oracle told me—
That if I did it no one could call me guilty,
But if I didn't, well, no arrow from a bow
Could shoot up to the heights of agony that would be mine.
Look at me. I am going now to his shrine,
Home of the center-stone and the undying flame,
Out of this place of blood.
There is nowhere else I can turn.
Listen, you people of Argos: remember how these agonies
came to be.
For a moment I was home; now I go to be what I always was:
A wanderer and an exile, in life and in death;
Leaving no legacy but the thing I did.

CHORUS

No, Orestes, you must not speak this way.
You did well; your act saved Argos;
(*The Furies appear to Orestes*)
You killed two serpents with a single—

ORESTES

NO!

Look at them!

They're black—and there are snakes around them—they—

CHORUS

Orestes, dearest son of your father,

What illusion is this?

Take hold of yourself. You have won the victory.

You have taken vengeance—

ORESTES

No—they are real. They stand there in the day.

I know what they are. They are the hounds of my mother.

CHORUS

They are visions, I tell you.

The blood that is still wet on your hands has shaken your brain.

ORESTES

Yes, the blood.
O God Apollo!
It's dripping out of their eyes!

CHORUS

Orestes, go to the shrine of Apollo as you had planned!

His touch will free you of this trouble.

ORESTES

You do not see them, but I do.

They drive me on—I can stay no longer—

(*Exit Orestes, pursued by the Furies*)

CHORUS

Good fortune to you, and may the god be kind to you.

Now has the third storm broken on this house of kings.
First was the Feast of Thyestes, fed with his children's flesh,
Next the death of the war-king, cut down in his bath,
And now has the savior—or avenger—come and gone.
When will it all end?
When will this harvest of hate be done
And the fury lie down and sleep?

ACT III

The Furies

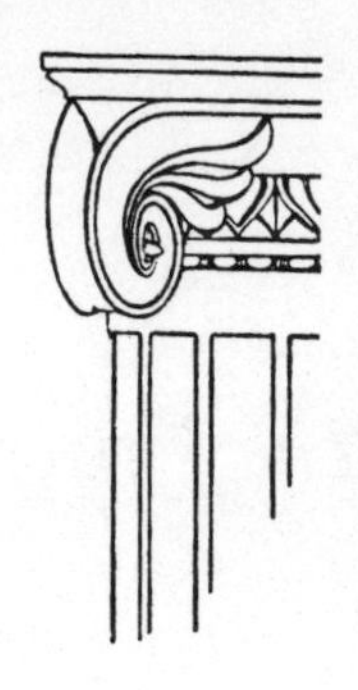

Characters

THE PYTHIA
APOLLO
HERMES
ORESTES
THE GHOST OF CLYTEMNESTRA
ATHENA
CHORUS OF FURIES
CITIZENS OF ATHENS

Scenes

Delphi: The shrine of Apollo. Athens: The shrine of Pallas Athena.

(In the inner sanctuary of the shrine of Apollo is Orestes, surrounded by sleeping Furies. Apollo himself and Hermes stand by him. This area is in shadow. An unlit brazier stands near on a tripod. The area before the temple is dimly lit as by early dawn. Enter here the Pythia, the priestess of Apollo.)

PYTHIA

I praise the dark Mother, the holy Earth,
First of all sybils, and that famous line
By which this seat of prophecy was given
To great Apollo.
He came from Delos to Parnassus' ground,
Sung on his way by the men of this land,
The masterful men who split the heart of the wilderness
With the straight spear of the road.
Here Zeus gave him the prophetic vision
And here, through me, he makes clear the cloudy will
of his father.
Here are the sacred precincts of gray-eyed Athena,
Here too the rock of Corycis, the bird-loud hollow,
walking place of gods.
Great Dionysus haunts this spot,
He whose worshipers, the wild white women, tore
King Pentheus
As eagles do the trapped and shivering hare.
I call upon the springs of Pleistus, the power of Poseidon,
And Zeus All-Father: inspire my mantic heart.
I go now to take my seat upon the sybil's throne,
And may the children of Hellas come before me, to hear the will
of the gods.
(She lights the brazier, and the inner shrine springs into light)

Ahh, God, God, God, the shrine is made a nest of terror,
And I broken from a holy priestess to a feeble old woman
With the frightened heart of a child.
Within is a man with the face of the god-hated,
Sitting upon the center-stone,
In one hand a blood-smeared sword,
In the other an olive-branch decked with fillets of wool
so white they glow, and before him—
Before him . . .
I saw in a picture once things like harpies or gorgons
So frightful they blasted the eyes, but these . . . these . . .
Black, wingless, bloated, utterly abominable,
The room full of the foul animal smell of their
sleeping breath,
Their eyes clotted with oozings of black blood . . .
I do not know what hole in the earth could bear these things
And not cry out in agony and sorrow.
I will not see more; a dreadful thing must run its course here,
And the house of great Apollo must be cleansed by
Apollo himself.
(*Exit the Pythia*)

APOLLO

(*to Orestes*)
I hold the power, and I will not forsake you.
Whether far or near, I stand your guardian to the end,
And my hand shall not weaken against your enemies.
See now, I have cast sleep upon these filthy creatures,
Handmaids of horror, wrinkled children of unreason,
Spawned by night and chaos, curled grublike in holes under
the earth, vessels of poison and darkness,
Loathsome alike to gods, and beasts, and men.
You must flee on, and they will be at your back,
But hope will drive your feet across the long leagues
of the earth,
And on the great water despair shall not be your shipmate.

You will come to sea-lapped cities, but only one will
  be your goal:
Athens, the home of Pallas.
There you will fall to earth, and embrace the knees of her
  ancient image,
And there you will find those who will render judgment
And speak powerful words, a spell of protection and peace.
This I swear: I who ordered you to strike down your mother.

ORESTES

Lord Apollo, you know what it means to do no wrong—
Can you understand what it means to take responsibility?
If so, no man need mistrust your will.

APOLLO

Let no doubt weaken your heart.
Hermes, my brother, they call you the god who guides;
Be so indeed to this man.
Have a care of him, for he is my suppliant, my—
  responsibility.
(*Exit Apollo, then Orestes led by Hermes. The Ghost of Clytemnestra appears.*)

CLYTEMNESTRA

Having a nice sleep, are you? Much good that does me.
I who walk dishonored among the other dead,
My disgrace does not sleep.
They call me manslayer and from their curses I find no rest.
No god takes *my* part, for all I suffered
From those I called my own.
There is a hole in my heart; think of where it came from.
Look at my scars with the inward eye
That sees in the darkness things unseen by day.
Remember that drink I poured for you by midnight,
That drink thicker and hotter than wine;
How you lapped it up at the hour unshared by gods—
All that is forgotten now, I see,
And your prey has skipped away like a young hare

From a pack of slow and stupid hounds.
Listen to me, you goddesses of the underworld;
I am pleading for my soul.
Listen to Clytemnestra crying in your dreams!
(*The Furies moan in their sleep*)
You may well whimper. He is on his way,
Guarded by friends who are no friends to me.
(*They moan again*)
I suffer, the mother-killer flies,
And your brains are too thick with sleep to care.
(*They moan again*)
Yes, you whine and then you fall back to sleep.
You've done nothing so far that wasn't wrong.
(*They moan again*)
Sleep and fatigue have mixed their drugs together;
The serpent's eye dims, and its coils relax.

CHORUS

Get him, get him, get him, get him—
After him!

CLYTEMNESTRA

You chase a beast of dreams, belling like hounds
That can't stop hunting even in their sleep.
What do you think you're doing?
Up! Get up
And shake yourselves awake!
Think of how you have failed, and let it dig
Into your hearts like a goad.
After him! Suffocate him with your blood-reeking breath!
Chase him! Pursue him! Wear him down to the bone!
(*Exit Clytemnestra*)

CHORUS

Wake, wake,
Up, up,
Out of the dark,
Come, come,

Ah, ah,
Up, up,
Wake, wake.
Aaaeee!
I hurt, I am pain,
He is running, he is gone,
We have not got him,
We were asleep.
Aah!
Son of Zeus, filthy sneak,
You have ridden down the gray old powers,
Loved the mother-killer, helped him escape.
Was this right? Was this right?

An accusation struck in my dreams
Like a gouge from a goad in the herdsman's fist;
Hard in the ribs, a hole in the heart,
Burning and freezing, it bites like a lash.

This is the way the young gods deal,
Blind-drunk with power, on a blood-slippery throne,
Slimed with blood from the head to the heel,
Stains on the stone at the center of earth.

The all-high seer fouls his own nest,
Hales on the rebellion, the heart-pride of man,
And breaks the lines of order drawn by the
gods of old.
He bedevils us now, but Orestes shall not escape;
Though he crawl in a hole in the earth, he will
find us breathing beside him;
With one curse cut off, another will push from
his flesh.

(*Apollo re-enters from his sanctuary*)

APOLLO

Leave this holy place, and leave at once,
Before a dart of light strikes like a silver snake

From the string of my golden bow,
And you roll in agony, puking the black blood
You have sucked from the hearts of men.
This is no resting place for such as you;
Go where you belong, to a stinking shambles
Where condemned men are wrestled to the block and the heads
Leap from their shoulders in a spout of blood,
Where the sex of young boys is crushed or cut away,
And men spiked under the spine with a greased stake
Are hoisted high to howl away their lives.
These are the things you love, that turn the stomachs of gods.
What you look like shows what you are.
Some hole in the rocks full of rotten flesh-scraps and dung of lions
Is where monsters like you belong,
Not mingling with worshipers in a holy shrine.
Get out, filth; go roam without guard or guide:
No self-respecting god would shepherd a flock like you.

CHORUS

My lord Apollo—if you have quite finished,
We too have a few things to say.
You are no mere accomplice in this crime—
If there is a crime—and there is—
The arch-criminal is you.

APOLLO

Explain that—and make it good.

CHORUS

It was by your oracle's command that this outlawed wanderer killed his mother.

APOLLO

I ordered him to avenge his father—what of it?

CHORUS

You promised him protection, still dripping with blood.

APOLLO

It was by my will that he came here
For purification and sanctuary, yes.

CHORUS

But we, who escorted him here, are abused and cursed.

APOLLO

No one asked for your presence in my house.

CHORUS

We are only doing our duty, my lord.

APOLLO

And what do you consider *that* to be?

CHORUS

Driving a matricide from place to place,
Allowing him no rest.

APOLLO

And who does the same to a woman who kills her husband?

CHORUS

That does not count. It is not kindred blood.

APOLLO

So? Then you count as nothing
The marriage of Zeus and Hera,
The pattern of all consummations?
You cast out of reckoning great Aphrodite,
From whom come the sweetest joys a man can know?
I tell you that the love of a man and wife
Transcends all oaths, and is watched over by Justice
As it was sealed by Fate.
If one of them can kill the other, and you wink your
    eye at it,
I say your pursuit of Orestes is not supported by right.
You whip yourselves into a fine froth over the one,
But to the other you are conveniently blind.
Well, we shall see. The goddess Pallas will judge.

CHORUS

Nothing will make me leave that man alone.

APOLLO

Go on, then. Give yourselves enough rope.

CHORUS

Do not try to talk me out of my ancient privilege.

APOLLO

Privilege? I would not have such "privilege" as a gift.

CHORUS

No, of course not; not the lily-pure Apollo
Who sits on the right hand of his father Zeus.
But a mother's blood drives *me,* and I shall have justice.
I go to track him down.
(*They exit*)

APOLLO

And I to protect him—for to betray a trust
Is among gods and men a monstrous thing.
(*He exits. The scene is now Athens. Some time has passed. Enter, to the shrine of Pallas Athena, Orestes, guided by Hermes.*)

ORESTES

Pallas Athena, Lady, I have come here by Apollo's command.
The stain of blood has faded,
But there is a great weight upon me.
I have been blown by the winds of the sea
And worn down by many roads.
I am very tired. I pray you receive me.
I will wait here for my judgment.

CHORUS

He is here—we are close upon him. Follow the
silent guides
Clear as the beads of blood that lead the hunting-pack
After the stricken fawn, to the place where the
quarry hides.
Orestes has gone to earth—follow upon his track!

By the welcome smell of blood I know he is near at hand . . .
Long with laboring lungs, blowing white spume from my lip,
At a man-killing pace have I ranged over endless oceans
    of land
And across the wide fields of water have followed his
    furrowing ship.

There! See him,
Cringing at the feet of Pallas' ancient image,
Blubbering for a trial and easy acquittal.
Not likely, that. It is not so simple
To bring a mother's blood that has soaked the earth
Back to her veins again.

Orestes, your turn has come; the wheel has turned again;
The sweet salt wine of your heart I will suck until,
    dry and white,
With nothing remaining of life but a mind that can
    still know pain,
I shall carry you out of the sun to the country
    of absent light.

There will you meet them all, the sinners of violent hand
Against god or guest or parent, brought here when they come
    to die;
For strictest of all accountants is the god of the underland,
And all old wrongs are tableted behind that watchful eye.

ORESTES

I have learned many things in the hard and bitter school
Of absolution. One is that there is a time to speak
And a time to keep silent.
This is a time to speak.
The stain of mother-murder is fading from my hand
And the blood sleeps.
I made sacrifice at the hearth of Apollo
While the blood was yet fresh and crying.
Since then, I have stood in the presence of countless men

And none of them has taken harm from me.
Time alters all things. It is from a pure mouth, I swear it,
That I call upon this country's guardian,
Holy Athena, to end this thing
Without more fall of blood.
Help me, great Goddess!
Wherever you may be, in the Libyan wilderness
Or by the waters of Triton, where you were born,
Whether marching to battle
Or sitting to take counsel and aid your friends,
Or standing terrible in arms overlooking the Phlegraean plain,
Hear me, gracious Lady, from far away:
Come, and deliver me from this thing that is upon me.

CHORUS

Never, never. No one will save.
Go down, go down, god-forsaken killer,
Bloodless shadow, gnawed by demons,
Hollow-hearted, go to the grave;
Go down, go down into the dark.

Come and join in the dance of hate,
Binding his soul with a terrible music:
Go down, go down, triple-damned Orestes,
Justice is pitiless, righteous, and straight;
Go down, go down into the dark.

Hold out your hands and if they are clean
You are safe from our anger and safe from our goad,
But if you have hidden them, knowing them stained,
You will find us in wait at the end of your road.

O Night my mother, O mother who bore me
To work out revenge on the blind and the seeing,
See how Apollo has scoffed at your laws
Ordained to endure to the end of all being,
Stolen to safety the shivering hare
Fattened for sacrifice under my claws.

Over the beast that is decked for the burning
Sing the song that eats at the brain,
Binding his soul with a terrible music;
The debt of outrage is paid with pain
Under the earth, and the worm is undying:
Go down, go down into the dark.

It is set down that none of the children of Heaven
Interfere in our dark and terrible office:
To pull down the pride and the guilt of great houses;
As we have no part in the rites of the gods,
In the robes blinding white in the sun, and the music.
For the work must be done that the children of Heaven,
The golden Immortals, will not soil their hands with:
To harrow the hearts of the killers of kinsmen,
Binding their souls with a terrible music.

All glories of men that rise high in the sunlight
Become as small dust as our shadow approaches
And our footbeats join in the dance of hate.
Hai! We come down like the fall of a mountain!
Let him run, let him run, for soon or late,
Though blinded with pride, the doer of evil
Shall feel us behind him, shall know we are with him
By a skin-rotting fog, by the closeness of darkness,
By a foulness about him, by the chill wind of fear, until
Hai! We come down like the fall of a mountain!

Let none who hear this dispute our will.
Despised by the gods, we yet play our parts:
Strength is ours, and wisdom, and skill,
Long memories, and implacable hearts.
Our way is set and ordained, and our right
Is old, as the darkness is older than light.
(*Enter Athena*)

ATHENA

From far away I heard your cry for aid;

By Scamander Water I stood, where the lords of Hellas
Gave over to my hand the land of Troy,
War-won, to be my domain forever.
I have come swiftly, on untiring feet,
My great cloak catching the hard-buffeting wind
And drawn by it as if by chariot horses.
Here I see an assembly bizarre to say the least,
That makes me wonder, but not fear.
Who in the world are you? All of you—
This stranger huddled up beside my image,
And you—whoever—or whatever, if I may use the word—
May *you* be? I must say that even a god
Who knows the form of every living thing on earth
Would be hard put to find *your* category.
Pardon me—I have no intention of being unkind;
Here, of all places, one should speak without prejudice.

CHORUS

Daughter of Zeus, you shall be told all, and briefly.
We are the daughters of eternal Night.
We are called the Curses in the land below the earth.

ATHENA

Very well, now I know your names and your parentage.
What next?

CHORUS

You shall soon learn our privileges and powers.

ATHENA

Splendid. Tell me everything.

CHORUS

When a man has killed another, we hound him from his home.

ATHENA

Where to? Has the chase no end?

CHORUS

Only in that place where joy is never heard of.

ATHENA

And is this what you are doing to this man?

CHORUS

Yes. He deliberately chose to murder his mother.

ATHENA

Freely? Wantonly? Or was he forced to do so
By fear of some greater punishment?

CHORUS

What could force a man to make such a terrible choice?

ATHENA

An excellent question. And his to answer, I think.

CHORUS

It's no good asking *him*. He won't be bound by oath.

ATHENA

You seem to be more concerned with the forms of justice
than the reality.

CHORUS

And what does *that* mean, pray?
Explain it out of your immense subtlety of mind.

ATHENA

Legal technicalities can be used to make wrong seem right.
That I will not allow.

CHORUS

Then examine him yourself, and give us an honest decision.

ATHENA

You will really trust my integrity, and abide by my judgment?

CHORUS

Why not? They say Nobility Obliges.
Perhaps Divinity will do the same.

ATHENA

Well, then. Stranger, it is your turn to speak.
Tell me your country and your parentage

And what trouble weighs on you, that you come a suppliant
to my hearth.
Remember that charges have been made against you which
must be answered.
I take it you have some faith in the soundness of your case
and the fairness of my judgment,
Or you would not be here at all.
Speak now, plainly and straightly.

ORESTES

Lady Athena, let me clear up one point.
I am not a suppliant, in the sense of some wretch craving
absolution from blood-guilt;
Your holy image took no pollution from the touch of my
hand.
I know that by law the man of blood is not even permitted
to speak in his own defense
Until he has been cleansed by ritual sacrifice.
This I have undergone. So much for that.
I am from Argos. For my parentage—
Thank you for asking, for I am proud to remember.
My father was Agamemnon, Captain-General and Lord
of the Fleet,
Your comrade-in-arms when you made Troy
A land without a city. He came home
To a squalid, dishonorable death.
My mother in the darkness of her heart
Tangled him in a robe as he came from his bath
And butchered him. I was in exile then,
But I came home, after long years.
And killed the woman who bore me. I do not deny it.
I took revenge because I loved my father,
But I also did it because Apollo
Promised me an existence of lively horror
If I failed to take blood for blood.
That is all I have to say.

I have put myself in your hands, and I will accept
your verdict
Whichever way it goes.

ATHENA

This is a matter of too far-reaching importance
For a mortal mind to decide.
I do not think that even I am qualified to judge
In a case where passionate anger was a motive.
Then too, you have declared yourself purified by holy ritual
And thrown yourself on my mercy,
And admittedly have done no harm to the city that is under
my protection.
I respect your rights,
But these, too, have their work to do,
And if they are robbed of their victory
The poison of their resentment will soak the soil of this land
And plague it, world without end.
It is a dilemma: whether I send them away or give them
their due
Someone will suffer for it.

Well, since it is my responsibility, and since a precedent is
being created here,
I shall establish for all time a court of law
To judge cases such as this one.
Make ready your proofs; call your witnesses
To substantiate your causes under oath.
I shall select the best citizens, and they too shall
be sworn
To judge this matter by nothing but the truth.
(*Exit Athena. Exit Orestes.*)

CHORUS

Unless we triumph
The old laws perish
And a Brave New Order
Shall reign instead,

Where parents' lives
Are spent in waiting
The day their children
Shall strike them dead.

Then we, who spy
On the guilt of mortals,
Will pour out wrath
On the heads of all:
Men shall seek false charms
From quacks and prophets
And see their doom
In their neighbors' fall.

Let no one cry
To *us* in anguish,
Broken by
Accidental woe;
Let none appeal
To the throne of Justice
When the house of Justice
Is fallen low.

There is need of fear
In the hearts of mortals;
It is well that knowledge
Is bought with sorrow:
No man today
Will stray from virtue
Who knows that Justice
May strike tomorrow.

Anarch and slave
Are both god-hated;
Safest of all
Is the middle way.
Daring and pride
Destroy that balance

That brings all good
For which men pray.

For him whose feet
Tread down the holy,
The shrine of Justice,
In hope of gain,
Who does dishonor
To guest or parent,
The gods make ready
Unheard-of pain.

Who sails with Justice
Without compulsion
Fair winds, calm waters
Will never fail,
While the laughing pirate
One day of darkness,
His mast storm-shattered,
Must strike his sail.

The blank sky deaf
To his anguished crying,
Who thought it clever
For such as he
To trust blind luck
And blinder Justice
Goes down to death
In the great blind sea.

(*Enter Athena, Apollo, Orestes, and Citizens*)

ATHENA

Proclaim order, herald. Let the hard bright blast of
the Etruscan trumpet,
Its brazen throat blown full with human breath,
Stab at the ear of this assembled host
And call them all to silence.
(*trumpet*)

It is best that attention be paid now,
For these new ordinances which I shall lay down
It is hoped will endure to the end of all being,
And this first case tried under them
Must be a model of fairness.

CHORUS

Lord Apollo, stick to your own bailiwick.
What right have you to meddle in this business?

APOLLO

I am here as a witness, because this man
Came to my hearth as a suppliant, and at my hands
Received absolution for the act of blood,
And also, in a sense, as co-defendant,
Because the ultimate responsibility for his mother's
death is mine.
(*to Athena*)
You know the rules, having made them. Begin the trial.

ATHENA

The prosecution has the right to open the case.
Let us know the truth of all that happened.

CHORUS

We are many, but our account will be concise.
Answer us point by point. Did you kill your mother?

ORESTES

Yes.

CHORUS

The first fall is ours.

ORESTES

But not the match.

CHORUS

Well. Then suppose you tell us *how* you slaughtered
your mother?

ORESTES

I took my sword and cut her throat.

CHORUS

And who prompted you to do this?

ORESTES

The oracle of Apollo. He will give testimony for me.

CHORUS

The prophet of a god ordered you to kill your own mother?

ORESTES

Yes. And even now I do not regret it.

CHORUS

When sentence is pronounced upon you, you will sing
a different song.

ORESTES

I am not afraid. My father will aid me from beyond
the grave.

CHORUS

Cut down your mother, and then put your trust in a corpse.
Straight thinking.

ORESTES

My mother was polluted twice over by her sin.

CHORUS

Perhaps you can explain that a little more clearly
to the court.

ORESTES

At one stroke she murdered her husband and my father.

CHORUS

If so, she has paid by her own death. Why should you not
do the same?

ORESTES

Why should *you* not have hounded *her* during her life of guilt,
as you have done with me?

CHORUS

Because the man she killed was not of her own blood.

ORESTES

Am I, then?

CHORUS

Murderer, she nourished you with her body! Do you deny you
were born of woman?

ORESTES

Lord Apollo, I call you now to give testimony.
Was there justice in my act, or was there none?
I do not ask you to deny that I did it, because I did.
I only ask: was I right to do it?

APOLLO

First let me assure you members of this court instituted
by Athena
That what I say to you will be based on justice only.
As a divine augur, I am bound to use no deceit.
No word has been spoken from my throne of prophecy
Concerning man or woman or city
That has not come from the All-Father, Olympian Zeus.
Consider this carefully. It means that what I say reflects
the will of the Father,
And no oath that may bind you is stronger than that.

CHORUS

And you maintain that your oracle
Was merely relaying the instructions of Zeus
In ordering Orestes to avenge his father
Regardless of dishonor to his mother?

APOLLO

Yes. How can you judge the two acts by the same rules?
A great lord of many battles,
Endowed by heaven with the royal scepter,
Cut down by a woman, and not even
By the fierce dart of an Amazon in fair fight—
You shall hear the manner of it,
You who sit in solemn judgment here.
He came home from the war, having achieved, as most
would agree,
A fair measure of success. She met him with a welcome

Fulsome in smooth graciousness,
And when he rose from his bath, naked and helpless,
She threw a great robe netlike over his head, tangled him
in its rich folds,
And cut him down.
That is how a great man died,
Pious, a good husband, loved by those he commanded.
I have described the woman's deed in naked terms,
Shown her to you for what she was,
To awaken righteous anger in you who will judge this case.

CHORUS

You claim that Zeus gives precedence to the rights
of a father.
But did not Zeus put his own father Kronos in chains?
Your argument contradicts itself.
I call upon the court to take note of this.

APOLLO

Filthy animals, creatures that sicken the gods,
Chains can be loosened, such a wrong can be set right
And no one is the worse.
But once the dust has drunk up a man's blood,
Once life has left him, there is no raising him to his
feet again.
That is one thing for which my father Zeus devised no cure,
Though otherwise he can turn the world over
Without a labored breath.

CHORUS

Well: consider the implications of your argument.
This man spilled his mother's blood into the dust.
Is he then to rest untroubled in his father's estate
in Argos?
What fellowship of worshipers will welcome him?
What altar is he to touch and not pollute?

APOLLO

I shall explain this too,

And you will see that right is on my side.
The mother is not the parent of what is called her child,
She is only the nurse, the matrix, the incubator of the seed
That is sown in her by the true parent, the man.
She is the stranger host who receives a stranger guest,
Shelters and feeds him for a time, and then,
If no god blight the seed,
Speeds him upon his way.
There can be fatherhood without a mother,
And as living proof of this I call to witness
Pallas Athena herself, daughter of Zeus,
Never nurtured in the darkness of the womb,
The goddess whom no goddess bore.

ATHENA

Apollo, you have made my task of blameless and impartial justice no easier.
Shall I assume now that enough has been said
And bid the jury render its verdict?

CHORUS

Our arrows have been shot. We wait for the decision.

APOLLO

You have heard what you have heard.
Cast your votes accordingly,
And keep in your hearts the oath that you have taken.

ATHENA

Listen now to my ordinance, people of Athens,
In this first trial for the act of blood.
On this hill, the Areopagus,
Shall succeeding generations assemble to see justice done,
And the authority of this court shall be passed on
To the end of all time.
Respect and devotion and healthy fear
Shall keep the hands of the citizens from evil
As long as justice and law remain uncorrupt;
For once the clear fountain is tainted with mire

Never more will its waters be quite fit to drink.
Let neither anarchy nor dictatorship be cherished among
you,
And do not banish fear entirely from the state,
For a man who fears nothing knows no law but his own
passion.
These things remembered may be to you
As a strong tower of protection over this city
Such as exists nowhere else among men.
I institute this court
Impersonal, incorruptible, severe,
A watcher in the night, an open eye in darkness.
I have spoken at length that all may hear
And take to heart these words when this day is over
And for all days to come.
Now must each man take his ballot, remember his oath,
And record his honest judgment.
I have said my say.
(*One at a time, the jurors scratch their votes on potshards and drop them in a single urn*)

CHORUS

Do not take our sisterhood lightly.
We can be a heavy weight on your land.

APOLLO

Remember the word of my oracle reflects the will of Zeus.
I advise you to let it come to fruition.

CHORUS

You honor acts of blood and meddle beyond your place.
The word of your oracle is corrupt and no longer valid.

APOLLO

Then my father Zeus was in the wrong
In receiving as suppliant Ixion, the first murderer?

CHORUS

Talk. But if justice is denied me
This land will never shake me from its back.

APOLLO

No one pays any heed to you,
Either among the elder gods or the younger. I shall win.

CHORUS

And abuse your victory, no doubt, as once before
When you tricked the Fates into letting a man escape death.

APOLLO

When a suppliant comes to me,
I believe in doing the right thing by him.

CHORUS

Especially when it gives you a chance
To mock the dignity of time-honored authority.
I remember how you muddled the wits of the ancient goddesses
with strong wine.

APOLLO

And I look forward to watching *you*,
Drunk with impotent rage, harmlessly puking your poison
When the verdict has gone against you.

CHORUS

Because I am old and you are young
You enjoy riding roughshod over me.
But I will await the verdict, and then I will know
Whether or not to let loose my rage upon this city.

ATHENA

The final judgment is mine,
And I shall explain how it will be made.
It is true that I was not born of woman,
And thus in all things I am the child of my father
And see things, admittedly, in the man's way.
A woman's natural loyalty is to her blood kin,
And she feels herself subject only to the law of her
own heart.
But a man must move not only in the home but in the world,
And is responsible not only to his own kind but to strangers.
His choices are not so easily made,

And since the woman in this case was not loyal even to her
own children,
I cannot find in her favor.
If the votes are equal, Orestes shall go on living.
Let the ballots be counted.

ORESTES

O bright Apollo, how will this end?

CHORUS

Black Night, my mother, are you watching this?

ORESTES

My hour has come: the noose or the light.

CHORUS

The end, or vindication of our dark powers.

APOLLO

Shake out the votes attentively, my friends,
And count them out with a painstaking care.
A lapse of judgment may bring disaster,
And one single vote save a great house from ruin.

ATHENA

The number of votes is equal on both sides.
I acquit this man of blood-guilt.

ORESTES

Pallas Athena, you have saved my house.
My country was lost to me and you have brought me home.
Now in Hellas men will say
"He is an Argive again,
And has returned to the estate of his father,
Thanks to wise Pallas and mighty Apollo
And that great Third who determines all things."
I go now, but first I pledge an oath
To you and your people, to endure for all time:
Never shall a ruler of Argos
Lead forth his armed men against Athens;
For if, as may be, we lie in the tomb of a hero-king,

We shall reach out our hand to strew their path
With evil omens, despair, and confusion.
But if they keep our covenant with the people of Athens
As friends in peace and companions in arms,
We shall touch them with grace from beyond the grave.
Farewell then, to you and to your people.
May you wrestle to a fall all those who come against you,
And may the wreath of victory crown your spears.
(*Exit Orestes*)

CHORUS

Aah, you upstart generation of gods,
You have crushed underfoot the laws of old time
And ripped my honored powers from my hands.
Now it is I who am disinherited, frustrated, abused;
But from my heart, sodden with anger,
As from a black cloud, I will rain poison on this land.
A crawling contagion—Justice! Justice!
White leprous foulness furring flesh,
Death to children and green leaves,
And ruin sweeping houses and fields like a broom.
I am mad with sorrow and mocked in my misery:
Daughters of darkness, what shall we do?

ATHENA

Listen to me, and restrain your anger.
You have not been as deprived of honor as you think.
A fair trial was held, and the balance of votes was equal.
The decision made came by the bright-burning word of
Zeus,
Interpreted through me and through Apollo,
That Orestes should not be only another drop to feed the
ocean of blood.
Let me persuade you not to visit your wrath upon poor men
Who have given you the respect and honor that is your due,
if you would only think about it,
As will *I*, if you will hear me.

CHORUS

That they could treat me so!
I, the ancient wisdom of the dark earth
Cast out like so much filth!
I shall do such things—
My rage chokes me, my breath hot and thick with anger—
Earth! Earth!
What agony crawls beneath my ribs?
O Night, mother Night, hear me:
They have made me a thing of scorn;
They, the clever tricksters, the new gods,
They who know nothing of honor have taken my honors away!

ATHENA

I am remaining patient with you, because you are my elders
And know many things that I will never know.
But I would not have you despise *my* wisdom altogether;
Nor my power—for Zeus has given me the keys to his
    dreadful treasuries of thunder,
Which I am unwilling but not unable to use.
You may find, in the fullness of time,
That you love this land better than you know,
And that it can be a hospitable home to you.
Why, then, gnaw its heart with fury and resentment,
Poisoning the blood of its young men with the
    wine of violence
Till they senselessly tear each other's flesh,
Fighting cocks of the same brood locked in a circled wall?
Let the spirit of war be turned outward, against the
    pride-drunk man
Who has fallen into the horrible love of glory.
There is room for both of us in this land;
For my shrine that towers in the light
And for yours in the caverns beneath the earth.
For each of us there will be shining thrones
Before a hearthside where the people come

To offer the first fruits of the harvest
And to pray for blessings on the seed that grows in the womb.

CHORUS

Let me understand this. What is this place you offer me?

ATHENA

A place where sorrow is never heard of. Please accept it.

CHORUS

And if I do accept it, is this mouth-honor, or shall
I have some power?

ATHENA

There will be life and joy in no house that is not touched
by your grace.

CHORUS

Do you mean this? Would you give me so important a place?

ATHENA

Both of us have our place in the lives of men.

CHORUS

You will remember this tomorrow, and the day after?

ATHENA

I would not promise what I do not mean to perform.

CHORUS

Your persuasion is strong. I feel a little less
angry already.

ATHENA

Stay here, then. You shall win other friends besides.

CHORUS

I am still of a mind to put a spell on this country.
What shall it be?

ATHENA

A spell of victories never arrived at by evil means;
A blessing that rises out of the soil like the gray
olive tree,
Leaps in blinding silver out of the sun-fired water,
Crosses the land with the breathing wind

Over the fat sleek beasts feeding in the meadow,
And circles the child growing beneath the mother's heart.
Let your power bring decay only to strangling and
parasitic weeds,
For like the gardener who works in love
I would bring to fruition the lives of the just and gentle.
This shall be your place. For me,
I shall see that the name of this city is held in honor
Throughout the world of men.

CHORUS

Then my home shall be here, beside you,
And my prayers for the good of your town:
That joy befall weddings and life attend birth
As the great sun to the ancient earth
Sends roots of radiance down.

ATHENA

It is indeed for the good of my people
That I give a place among them
To these goddesses, so violent and so difficult to reconcile.
For their workings are to be seen in the heart of
every human act,
And the man who denies them will be torn by forces beyond
his understanding
And the sins of his parents against them
May encircle him unperceived
Until, too late, he cries, "What have I done?" and they,
Not dignifying him with an answer, batter him to dust.

CHORUS

Great Pan, against the black wind
Protect the young green leaves
While the double wealth of herd and vine
And the glowing yield of the deep mine
Athena's city receives.

ATHENA

Guardians of this city, hear these words

And the promise they convey.
Great is the power of these, the Furies,
Both among the gods and among the nations of the dead,
But among men their power is absolute
And as they dispose, so must it be;
Singing for some, for others, the eye dimmed with tears.

CHORUS

I pray for no more youth
To perish before its prime;
That Revenge and iron-hearted War
May fade with all that has gone before
Into the night of time.

ATHENA

Why, now you speak good words,
Words of life and peace,
And I salute the power of patient Persuasion, by which this has come about.
I see in these once terrible faces
Great good, great blessing for all who give them due honor
And deal justly with them, as I have done.

CHORUS

Long be your city's years
And wisdom and joy your part.
Farewell: your destiny is great
If you can learn to love and hate
With a united heart.

ATHENA

Farewell, ancient children of Night. Go now to your home,
Led by me and guided by the people of this land,
Purple-robed, bearing the dancing fire
Of ceremonial torches.
To the primal caverns under the holy hill,
With solemn sacrifice, blessed and blessing,
With praise and great honor, go to your home.

CHORUS

Farewell. Farewell.

ATHENA

And you, people of my city:
For the good of all men a compact has been made
Between the power of Zeus and the power of Fate,
Between the light of the mind and the voices of the blood.
Think of these things in silence.

CHORUS OF ATHENIAN CITIZENS

Now to the caverns of night,
Honored and praised, by the fire of the torches,
Daughters of Earth
Whose name is mystery,
Blessed and blessing
Go to your homes.

Lead them with singing and light,
Honor and praise to their mercy and justice;
Men of the earth,
Think on this mystery:
Blessed and blessing
Go to your homes.

(*Exeunt Omnes*)